Teacher's Manual

Teacher's Manual

for

Declaration Statesmanship

A Course in American Government

Richard Ferrier, Ph.D.
Andrew Seeley, Ph.D.

Fourth Edition

Fourth Edition

Authored by Richard Ferrier and Andrew Seeley

Cover design by: Caroline Green
Cover image: Declaration of Independence (1819), oil on canvas, John Trumbull (1756–1843), public domain via Wikimedia Commons.

ISBN: 978-1-5051-2270-1

Published in the United States by
TAN Books
PO Box 269
Gastonia, NC 28053
www.TANBooks.com

Printed in India

Contents

Introduction

Required Course Materials:

- *Declaration Statesmanship: A Course in American Government* Student Text (ST)
- *Declaration Statesmanship: A Course in American Government* Book of Readings (BR)
- *Declaration Statesmanship: A Course in American Government* Teacher Manual (TM)
- *Declaration Statesmanship: A Course in American Government* Streaming Video Lectures

The Student Text (ST) contains the main text for this course as well as the Questions for Reflection and Chapter Review Questions referred to in the lesson plan.

The Book of Readings (BR) includes all primary texts required by the lesson plan.

This Teacher's Manual (TML) contains lesson plans, chapter outlines, strategies for teaching the textbook material, quizzes, tests, and all answer keys for Questions for Reflection, Chapter Review Questions, and tests and quizzes.

The video lectures elaborate on the content in both the Student Text (ST) and Book of Readings (BR) and connect different themes and questions to enrich students' understanding of key concepts and ideas.

The lesson plans assume the student will spend 1 - 2 hours daily, four days a week, for 15 weeks on this course. This plan allows flexibility on the fifth day of each week (typically Fridays) to complete lengthier assignments or pursue supplemental readings or activities suggested in the textbook. Most high school courses run 16-weeks to the semester, so you also have the option of spreading some work out over a longer period of time.

Note: It is not part of this course to assign extensive reading in history books or great literature, but we have also taught it over two semesters as a combined history and civics course. You may opt to attempt that using a trustworthy reading list as well.

Suggested Supplemental Reading

- Samuel Eliot Morison's *The Oxford History of the American People*, 1965 (a book widely available second-hand), chapters 12 to 14, for the preliminaries to the American Revolution, chapters 18 to 20, for forming American governments, and chapters 44 to 48, for the period of Reconstruction through McKinley.
- James M. McPherson's *Battle Cry of Freedom*, 1988, chapters 1 to 8, for the Missouri Compromise and the road to the Civil War (chapter 7 in our text).

Lesson Plan

To make the most of this important course, we suggest the following:

1. Follow the schedule to complete the material in a timely fashion. By keeping on schedule, you will complete this course in one semester. If, however, you want to use the supplemental texts and spread the course out over a full year, then you have that flexibility.
2. As this is a high school course, we recommend that you take notes as you read and watch the video lectures. Outlining the chapters *and* answering the Questions for Review as assigned are two ways to fix the ideas, documents, and key events in your memory.
3. Complete and check your answers to the Questions for Review thoroughly. These will help you know whether you have grasped the central ideas of the chapter. Also read the "Order of Events" carefully at the end of each chapter: this resource will give you context for the development of American government over time.
4. For tips on customizing this course, be sure to talk to your parents about scheduling a consult with your TAN Academy coach.
5. The plans below refer to the course components as follows:

    - Student Text: ST
    - VID: Streaming lecture
    - Book of Readings: BR
    - Teacher's Manual: TML

Week 1

Day 1

- ST: read the Introduction, pp. 1 - 5; answer the Chapter Review Questions
- VID: watch Lecture 1 and take notes
- BR: read The Declaration of Independence and The Gettysburg Address
- Other: begin memorizing the Gettysburg Address (due Day 5)
- TML: Comments on, and suggested answers for, many of the Questions for Reflection can be found in part 4 of this manual.

Day 2

- VID: watch Lecture 2 and take notes
- BR: read Federalist No. 1
- Other: continue memorizing the Gettysburg Address
- TML: Do Questions on the Readings #1-3 and "General Discussion," p. 68

Day 3

- ST: read Chapter 1, pp. 7 - 11 (to and including Order of Events I); do the Chapter Review Questions 1–3 and complete the Timeline Exercise to organize the events discussed in the the text.
- BR: read Federalist No. 9 (up to the point indicated Questions on the Readings #1–2)
- Other: continue memorizing the Gettysburg Address

- TML: Do Questions on the Readings #1-3 and "General Discussion," p. 72

Day 4

- ST: read Chapter 1, pages 12 to 14 (up to "Reasons for Independence"); do Chapter Review Question 4
- BR: read Thucydides' "Melian Dialogue"
- Other: Recite the Gettysburg Address from memory for a parent or tutor.

Week 2

Day 1

- ST: read Chapter 1, pp. 14 - 22 (to end of chapter)
    - *Note: in this and all ST assignments the Order of Events and Questions for Reflection are part of finishing a chapter; always plan to complete these after you reach the end of the chapter
- BR: *optional:* read the Magna Carta, English Bill of Rights, and *Common Sense* (Thomas Paine)
- Other: read "Paper Topic 1" on p. 24 in ST; outline your paper (due Week 3, Day 1)

Day 2

- ST: read Chapter 2, pp. 27 - 33 (through the material for Question for Reflection 2)
- VID: watch Lecture 3 and take notes
- Other: begin memorizing the Declaration of Independence (exclude the list of charges against the king); the upcoming test schedule is as follows:

Day	Section
Week 2, Day 3	1st paragraph
Week 2, Day 4	2nd paragraph
Week 3, Day 1	3rd - 5th paragraphs
Week 3, Day 2	From "in every stage" to "connections and correspondence"
Week 3, Day 3	From "they, too" to "publish and declare"
Week 3, Day 4	entirety

Day 3

- ST: finish Chapter 2 and do the Questions for Reflection
- BR: Jefferson's First Draft of the Declaration, p. 70
- Other: Recite the first paragraph of the Declaration. Write the rough draft of your paper.

Day 4

- BR: read Calvin Coolidge, "The Inspiration of the Declaration"
- Other: Recite the second paragraph of the Declaration. Review your paper and make edits for content and clarity.
- TML: do Questions on the Readings, p. 96

Week 3

Day 1

- ST: read Chapter 3, pp. 35 - 40 (stop before "Catholic Witness"); do Chapter Review questions #1–7
- Other: Paper Topic 1 due (final draft). Recite paragraphs 3–5 of the Declaration.

Day 2

- ST: read Chapter 3, pp. 40 - 42 (through Question for Reflection 5)
- VID: watch Lecture 4 and take notes
- Other: Recite the Declaration from "In every stage" to "connections and correspondence"

Day 3

- ST: read Chapter 3, pp. 43 - 47 ("Aristotle" and "Cicero"); do Chapter Review questions #8 - 12
- BR: read Aristotle, *Ethics*, Book I, Ch. VII
- Other: Recite the Declaration from "They too" to "publish and declare"

Day 4

- ST: read Chapter 3, pp. 47 - 55 (to end of chapter); do remaining Chapter Review questions and review the timeline
- BR: read Locke, *Second Treatise on Government*, Ch. II
- Other: Recite the remaining paragraphs of the Declaration

Day 5

- Study for Quiz 1 on the Declaration (Quiz Week 4, Day 1)

Week 4

Day 1

- ST: read Chapter 4, pp. 57 to 63; do Chapter Review questions #1 - 5
- BR: read "Declaration of the Immediate Causes Which Induce and Justify the Secession of South Carolina from the Federal Union"
- TML: Take Quiz 1 closed book and closed notes, then correct with a parent to assess your mastery

Day 2

- ST: read Chapter 4, pp. 63 - 67; do Chapter Review question #6 and Questions for Reflection #2, p. 63
- BR: *optional:* read Jefferson, "Summary View of the Rights of British America",
- Thomas Hutchinson, "Strictures Upon the Declaration"

Day 3

- ST: read Chapter 4, pp. 68 - 71
- Read Paper Topic 2, p. 72, and begin your outline (due Week 5, Day 3)
- VID: Watch Lecture 5 and take notes

Days 4 & 5

- **Study for Test 1:** The test in the next lesson will cover all the material assigned so far (including those from the Book of Readings). Use the questions and outlines to help your students prepare. Be sure to review the major historical facts that are referred to in the text. Also go over the memorized sections from the Gettysburg Address and the Declaration.
- Other: using your outline, write the rough draft of your paper on Topic 2

Week 5

Day 1

- TML: Take **Test 1** (closed book, closed notes); have a parent or tutor score the test, circling any incorrect answers, then go back through the text and your notes to correct them

Day 2

- VID: Watch Lecture 6 and take notes
- BR: read the Articles of Confederation
- Other: re-read the draft of your paper for Topic 2 and make edits for content and clarity
- TML: do Questions on the Reading, p. 60

Day 3

- ST: read Chapter 5, pp. 73 - 79; Chapter Review questions #1 - 3
- Other: Paper Topic 2 (final draft) due

Day 4

- VID: Watch Lecture 7 and take notes
- BR: read The Constitution: Preamble and Article I
- Other: memorize the Preamble to the Constitution
- TML: do Questions on the Reading, #1 - 6, p. 62

Day 5

- Other: finish memorizing the Preamble

Week 6

Day 1

- BR: read The Constitution: Articles II–VII
- Other: Recite the Preamble
- TML: do Questions on the Reading, #7 - 11, p. 62

Day 2

- BR: read The Constitution, Amendments I–XXVII
- Other: begin memorizing Amendments I, IX, X, and XIV
- TML: do Questions on the Reading, #1 - 8, p. 66

Day 3

- BR: read Federalist No. 2

- Other: finish memorizing Amendments I, IX, X, and XIV; review for **Quiz 2**
- TML: do Questions on the Reading, p. 70

Day 4

- BR: read Federalist No. 15, and No. 16 up to the point indicated in the Book of Readings*
- Other: Recite Amendments I, IX, X, and XIV
- TML: Take **Quiz 2**, closed book, closed notes; do Questions on the Reading, p. 74

*Note: For those not using our Book of Readings, Federalist No. 16 should be read up to the end of the paragraph that begins, "The result of these observations. . . "

Week 7

Day 1

- ST: read Chapter 5, pp. 79 - 88; do Chapter Review questions #4 - 9**
- VID: Watch Lecture 8 and take notes
- BR: read "Washington's Letter of Transmittal to the President of the Continental Congress"

**Note: Take some time to think about Questions for Reflection 2 and 3. The debate over the powers of the federal government began with the first Congress, and has not stopped since. It will be invaluable to see what two of the drafters of the Constitution thought.

Day 2

- ST: read Chapter 5, pp. 88 - 95; do Chapter Review questions #10 - 11***
- VID: Watch Lecture 9 and take notes
- BR:
- Other:
- TML:

***Note: Questions for Reflection 8 encourages the student to draw connections between the Declaration and the Constitution.

Day 3

- ST: read Paper Topic 3, p. 105; outline your paper and begin your rough draft (due Week 8, Day 3)

Day 4

- ST: read Chapter 5, pp.s 95 - 104; do Chapter Review questions #12 - 16
- BR: read Federalist No. 84
- Other: finish your rough draft of Topic 3
- TML: do Questions on the Reading, p. 76

Week 8

Day 1

- **Study for Test 2.** Test 2 will cover Chapter 5 as well as the assigned readings. Use the questions and outlines to help students review the Articles and the Constitution. Be sure to review the powers and qualifications of the three branches of our government and the procedure for making laws. Make sure students are familiar with the contents of the first ten amendments.

Day 2

- Other: edit your rough draft for content and clarity
- TML: **Take Test 2** (closed book, closed notes); have a parent or tutor score the test, circling any incorrect answers, then go back through the text and your notes to correct them

Day 3

- ST: read Chapter 6, pages 107 to 113; do Chapter Review questions #1 - 4
- BR: read the Northwest Ordinance
- Other: Topic 3 paper (final draft) due

Day 4

- ST: read Chapter 6, pp. 113 - 120; do Chapter Review questions #5 - 7
- spend extra time today on Questions for Reflection #1 - 2; if possible, discuss with a parent or tutor
- VID: Watch Lecture 10 and take notes

Week 9

Day 1

- ST: read Chapter 6, pp. 120 - 124; finish the Chapter Review questions and review the Timeline
- BR: read the Cornerstone Speech; *optional*: read Calhoun's "Speech on the Oregon Bill"
- TML: do the Questions on the Reading, p. 94

Day 2

- ST: read Chapter 7, pp. 125 - 135 (to the end of the speech)
- VID: watch Lecture 7 and take notes

Day 3

- ST: read Chapter 7, pp. 135 - 140; do Chapter Review questions #1 - 2

Day 4

- ST: do Chapter 7 Review question #3; outline your answer and write a full reflection essay grounded in historical evidence*

*Notes: Question 3 will take some time, but will greatly help students understand the material of this chapter. They might need to use a history book or an encyclopedia. You may want to extend the exercise over several days.

Week 10

Day 1

- BR: read the Peoria Speech, part 1*
- TML: do the Questions from Readings #1 - 5, p. 82

*Note: for those not using our Book of Readings, that is up to the paragraph beginning, "I think, and shall try to show, that it is wrong. . . "

Day 2

- ST:
- VID:
- BR: read the Peoria Speech, part 2**
- TML: do the Questions from Readings #1 - 5, p. 84

**Note: up to the paragraph beginning,"But one great argument in support of the repeal. . . "

Day 3

- BR: read the Peoria Speech, part 3 (conclusion)
- TML: do the Questions from Readings #1 - 4 and Questions for General Discussion #1 - 2, p. 84

Day 4

- ST: read Chapter 7, pp. 143 - 153; do the Chapter Review questions #4 - 6
- BR: read the Lincoln-Douglas debates, 6th Debate

Week 11

Day 1

- ST: read Chapter 7, pp. 153 - 163; do the Chapter Review questions #7 - 9

Day 2

- VID: watch Lecture 12 and take notes
- BR: read Speech On the Dred Scott Decision; *optional:* read *Dred Scott v. Sandford*
- TML: do the Questions from Readings #1 - 5, p. 88

Day 3

- ST: read Chapter 7, pp. 163 - 174; do Chapter Review question #10
- BR: read Lincoln's Second Inaugural Address
- Other: **Review for Quiz 3** on American policy regarding slavery, found in this manual Review: This chapter is the most involved of the whole book. Use this lesson for review, additional discussion of Questions for Reflection, and discussion of the theme of Lincoln's Declaration Statesmanship.

Day 4

- TML: Take **Quiz 3** closed book, closed notes. Ask a parent to score your first attempt, then use your texts and notes to correct any missed questions.

Week 12

Day 1

- ST: read Chapter 8, pp. 177 - 189; do Chapter Review questions #1 - 4
- Other: review the Gettysburg Address, which you memorized at the beginning of this class; refresh your memory!

Day 2

- ST: read Chapter 8, pp. 189 - 201; do Chapter Review questions #5 - 7
- BR: read the Open Letter to Pres. McKinley by the Colored People of Massachusetts
- Other: review the Gettysburg Address

Day 3

- ST: read Chapter 8, pp. 201 to 214; finish Chapter Review questions and review the Timeline
- BR: read Booker T. Washington's "The Case of the Negro"; *optional*: read Niagra's Declaration of Principles

Day 4

- VID: watch Lecture 13 and take notes
- Other: begin reviewing for **Test 3**. Test 3 will cover Chapters 6–8 as well as the assigned readings from the Book of Readings. Use the review questions and outlines to help review. Be sure you know the major historical facts that affected the Declaration policies of the founding fathers, Lincoln, and Martin Luther King, Jr. (e.g. Northwest Ordinance, Missouri Compromise, Kansas-Nebraska Act, the Dred Scott decision, the Thirteenth, Fourteenth, and Fifteenth Amendments, Jim Crow laws, Plessy v. Ferguson, Brown v. Board of Education, and the Civil Rights Act of 1964).

Week 13

Day 1

- Other: Study for **Test 3**

Day 2

- TML: Take **Test 3** (closed book, closed notes); have a parent or tutor score the test, circling any incorrect answers, then go back through the text and your notes to correct them

Day 3

- BR: read Tocqueville, first reading*
- TML: do Questions on the Readings #1 - 8, p. 78

*Note: for those not using our Book of Readings, that is *Democracy in America*, Vol. 1, Ch. XVII, subsections titled "Indirect influence of religious opinions upon political society in the United States", "Principle causes which render religion powerful in America," and "How the education, the habits, and the practical experience of Americans promote the success of their democratic institutions"; or in some editions, Vol. I, Part Two, Chapter 9, similar three subsection titles

Day 4

- BR: read Tocqueville, second reading**
- TML: do Questions on the Readings #1 - 8, p. 80

**Note: for those not using our Book of Readings, that is *Democracy in America,* Vol. 2, Second Book, Ch. IV and V; or in some editions, Vol. II, Part Two, Ch. 4 and 5

Week 14

Day 1

- ST: read Chapter 9, pp. 215 - 220; do Chapter Review questions
- Other: review the Declaration of Independence, which you memorized earlier in this course; brush up on your memory work!

Day 2

- ST: read Chapter 9, pp. 220 - 227; do Questions for Reflection #1 - 4, p. 227
- Review the Preamble to the Constitution, which you memorized earlier in this course; brush up on your memory work!

Day 3

- ST: read Chapter 9, pp. 228 - 234; finish the Chapter Review questions
- VID: Watch Lecture 14 and take notes

Day 4

- ST: read the Epilogue, pp. 235 - 245
- Other: choose one of the Questions for Reflection from p. 234 and outline a 5 paragraph essay answering it in full; alternatively, compose a 2 - 3 page response to the authors' final question at the end of the Epilogue: "What should we, the citizens, do now?" for either option, this is your final assignment of the year. Plan to quote the various statesmen you have studied in support of your statements and opinions.

Week 15

Day 1

- Other: write your rough draft of the final essay using the outline you composed last week

Day 2

- Other: if needed, add direct quotations from the statesmen you have read this year to bolster your argument

Day 3

- Other: Edit your paper for content, clarity, and sound argument

Day 4

- Other: final draft of final essay due

Teaching Strategies

Introduction: The Declaration of America

The aim of this course is to educate students about the importance of the Declaration of Independence for America and bring them to understand the principles contained in that great document. The introduction expresses the view of the authors on the importance of the Declaration: It is the document 1) that formally began our existence as a nation, 2) that contains the principles on which our nation was founded, and 3) to which the country must return in moments of crisis. The marriage analogy brings out these three aspects. The wedding vows 1) formally begin the marriage, 2) contain the principal promises on which the relationship is founded, 3) and are those to which the married couple must return in times of difficulty.

In our teaching experience, we have found that the first and often most difficult task of teaching is to remove erroneous views that students have assimilated from different sources. So, a good part of this book is devoted to clearing up misconceptions that have crept into many Americans' understandings of the Declaration and founding of the country. One important error is to think that the country was founded by the Constitution, and the Declaration has nothing do with our nation's law. The primacy of the Declaration is evident from our traditions, laws, and the Constitution itself. We will see further evidence for this in later chapters, especially chapter 5, on the Articles of Confederation and Constitution.

The teacher should lead the students through the first three Questions for Reflection to firmly establish that the United States began with the Declaration. You might also bring up the fact that the official U.S. Code of Law lists the Declaration as the first document. Another fact that points to the importance of the document is that we date our founding from July 4, 1776, not July 2. On July 2, Congress passed a resolution declaring separation; on July 4, they approved the document as the formal declaration of independence. It is from the day of the document's acceptance that we date our country.

The importance of this point cannot be overstated. The Declaration states that our nation is founded in immutable laws of human nature established by God, which laws judge the legitimacy of government. The Constitution, a practical document meant to structure a government based on these principles, does not explicitly restate these principles. Those who date our country from 1789 tend to think that the will of the majority is the ultimate source of justice, answerable to no other.

Of course, you don't have to explain all this to the students now. You will see the argument developed over the course of this part of the book. However, you should make sure that the students see all the evidence pointed out here.

The marriage analogy is very helpful for understanding the political reality of the founding of the nation. In many ways, the American nation formed gradually into a cultural and political union. Originating and functioning more or less as separate entities for over a century, the colonies began uniting politically around the 1750s. The 1750s to early 1770s might be considered the period of political courtship, while the First Continental Congress would be an engagement. The Articles of Confederation and the Constitution were like different attempts at arranging household responsibilities.

But the formal solemnization of the union was brought about by the Declaration of Independence. Until that time, each colony had a separate legal bond to the English sovereign. The Declaration dissolved those bonds and established the new bonds of the states in one Union.

You might note the importance of the *Federalist Papers.* This collection of essays urging New York to ratify the Constitution is still considered the most authoritative interpretation of the Constitution ever written. We will be referring to it throughout this part of the book, so you might want to make your students familiar with it.

Chapter One — A Look Backwards

Outline of Chapter 1

I. The colonies vs. Parliament [1.1]
   A. Parliament attempted to govern the colonies directly by levying taxes and passing laws
   B. The colonies denied Parliament's claims and resisted its measures
   C. Parliament and the King declared the colonies to be in rebellion
II. The Americans hesitate to declare independence [1.2]
   A. Americans feared the bad reputation of democracy
   B. The injustice of Athenian democracy ("tyranny of the majority")
   C. The instability of ancient democracies
III. Reasons for independence [1.3]
   A. Americans came to believe that George was a tyrant
      1. British history of resisting tyrants
         a. Traditional limitations on the power of the king
         b. 16th century: English kings dominated Parliament

c. 17th century: while Americans ruled themselves through colonial legislatures, Parliament reasserted its supremacy over the king

2. Americans hoped for a just and stable popular goverment
   a. They thought government should be ordered to justice and happiness rather than based on power
   b. Political philosophy and the Bible taught them this
3. King George was a tyrant
   a. Parliament attempts to rule the colonies directly
   b. King George encourages Parliament
   c. *Common Sense* argues that all monarchy leads to tyranny

This chapter is not a history, but a cursory review and interpretation of certain historical events that provide background to the Declaration. To better grasp the history, we strongly recommend that the teacher read relevant chapters from Clarence B. Carson's book, *The Rebirth of Liberty*, or Samuel Eliot Morison's *Oxford History of the American People*, chapters 12–14.

Besides providing background for the Declaration, this chapter has for a primary aim removing some misconceptions about the causes of the Revolutionary War. Certain common views imbibed by students either deny the justice of the colonists' decision to fight or trivialize their nobler sentiments into masks covering a bald-faced power grab. These views are usually based on a poor understanding of the political situation of the colonists, or pernicious theoretical views of human nature (e.g., that men only care about money and power). In this chapter, we try to show that men can and sometimes do act for noble motives.

A very common view is that the British government, king and Parliament, had always made laws governing the colonies. However, because of internal problems in Britain and the financial success of the colonies, the colonies enjoyed a century of "Salutary Neglect," during which Britain did not exercise its authority over internal colonial matters. The colonists, having grown used to their freedom, were unwilling to accept interference, even in the form of a minor taxation from the government which had protected them during the French and Indian War. They had conceived novel ideas of freedom which would lead to the Revolution.

The first and third parts of the chapter attempt to show that Britain, particularly the British Parliament, tried to change its relationship to the colonies and overthrow centuries of British tradition. The issue of taxation, which was one of a number of acts that attempted to assert Parliament's supremacy over the colonists, was an issue of freedom, not of financial burden.

Their knowledge of Britain's own experience had shown that, without having the power of approving taxation, the guarantees of freedom given them by the government were only as good as the paper they were written on.

The second part of the chapter, on ancient democracies, provides important background for understanding the Constitution as an instrument of freedom. Democracy had historically failed for two main reasons. One, it was considered rule of the majority, by the majority and for the majority. It did not base itself on the God-given equality of men, but on the power of the masses to dominate the elite. This is like the positive law view which many have of our own Constitution, which recognizes no higher idea of justice than the will of the majority, no standard by which that will can be itself judged. We strongly recommend reading the "Melian Dialogue" from Thucydides in this regard. Two, democracies were notoriously unstable because of the fickleness of the people. We see how changeable opinion polls are in our day. In ancient democracies, a mass gathering that was the equivalent of an opinion poll enacted law. As we will see, the Constitution's checks and balances are aimed as much at preventing a hastily-put-together majority from dominating the nation, as at preventing bold men from grabbing power.

Two other misconceptions might cause difficulty for the student in understanding this chapter. Many scholarly works and textbooks on our founding criticize America for claiming equality for all men, while continuing to keep black slaves, and treating freed blacks, women and Indians unjustly. However, our general position on the founders is that they were nobly-motivated men, who were burdened by sin as we all are, and who inherited with slavery a very difficult situation. But by laying the foundations of the country on the principles of the Declaration, they intentionally sowed the seeds for the ultimate end of slavery.

Another view often held about our founding is that religion had nothing to do with it. Our country's founding, it is held, was the act of atheistic or deistic rationalists like John Locke. That this is a distortion of the reality will be shown in chapter 3.

Chapter Two — The Declaration Itself

In this chapter, the students are to read and discuss the actual text of the Declaration. The exercises in this chapter are crucial for the proper development of the student's understanding of the Declaration. Once students are put in direct contact with this great document, they will be able to engage some of the common misrepresentations of it. The rest of this part of the book will be offering a straightforward, but academically controversial, reading of the Declaration. The students should be familiar enough with the document to see that we are reading the text, not making it say what we want. Depending on the students' desires and your own time limits, you might want to spend a couple of classes on the discussion.

The students should attempt Question for Reflection 1, the outline, on their own before they come to class. It is crucial for the students to see that the Declaration presents an argument, with a series of universal premises, a long list of particular facts related to those premises, and the practical conclusions drawn. The founders wanted it to be known that their actions were based on universal maxims of justice, and not simply on the passions of the moment.

In our experience discussing the Declaration with high school and college students, we have found many students have difficulty recognizing the difference between an argument and mere desire-driven opinion. The last two centuries have left many of us with the impression that both contemporary and historical political figures only use arguments as smokescreens in their quest for power.

The best antidote to this is to focus on what is said in the Declaration. The Declaration is important for our country in the ideals and principles it puts forth, and the founders' hidden motives are unknowable and irrelevant for our purposes. Also, it is not only pious but reasonable to assume that those who risked their possessions and their lives are at least as good as, if not better than, ourselves.

One particular difficulty that students often face in this regard is the meaning of "men." The founders said, "All men are created equal," but, it is claimed, they obviously didn't mean that to apply to the black slaves. Certainly some did not, but in the second part of the book we will argue that most, including many slaveholders, did in fact mean it to apply to slaves, and their universal statement here in the founding document led to the ultimate destruction of slavery and the protection of the civil rights of blacks and others. However, if you have your students read the paragraphs about slavery that were a part of Jefferson's draft, you can see at least what he thought of it.

The students should think about Questions for Reflection 3 (on God) and 4 (on the branches of government) and discuss them.

Chapter Three — The Roots of American Liberty

Outline of Chapter 3

I. Biblical teaching is an important source of the Declaration's principles [3.1]

  A. The Bible teaches that:
    1. All men are created equal
    2. This truth is written on the hearts of all men
  B. Faithful witnesses
    1. Calvin Coolidge argued that the equality of all men follows from the universal Fatherhood of God
    2. Colonial preachers taught the equality of men, the origin of the civil power in the people, and the right to replace tyrants
    3. The Catholic theologians argued that, because all men are equal, just government comes from the consent of the governed

II. The teaching of political philosophers formed American views of liberty, justice and good government [3.2]
  A. Aristotle taught that:
    1. All men have the same nature
    2. Men naturally want to live together in society
    3. The best kind of government is one in which all classes of men share in governing
    4. Justice exists by nature
    5. True happiness comes from virtuous action
  B. Cicero taught that:
    1. Natural law is higher than man-made law
    2. All men are equal, because they can equally know the natural law
  C. John Locke taught that:
    1. Before governments exist, all men are equal and subject to the law of nature
    2. Government is needed to establish justice, and arises from the consent of the governed
    3. Tyranny should be resisted by the people

This chapter aims to explain briefly what Jefferson meant in the quotation on page 43 about the common opinions that the Declaration intended to express as the basis for revolution. Jefferson thought these opinions to be matters of common sense. He dared to call them "self-evident" in the Declaration. Americans had common sense views about the importance of freedom and equality, and they found those views supported in many different quarters.

Many mistaken interpretations of the Declaration have been made because of exclusive emphasis on one aspect of the thought of the founders. The most common these days is the exclusively rationalist view. In this view, the Declaration is simply the expression of the political philosophy of the Rationalists, especially John Locke, who rejected or minimized faith and revelation. On the other hand, there is also a temptation, partly in reaction to the former position, to hold that the Declaration is so based in Christianity as to be unintelligible apart from faith in Christ.

This chapter attempts to show in a brief way the many different sources of American thought on equality, the natural law and the origin of government. The first part takes its direction from the three opening quotations. The first quotation shows God's revelation of the universal dignity and equality of men; the second shows that God has revealed that this truth can be known by all men without special revelation; the third is the Declaration's position that this truth is "self-evident," because of natural reason and revelation. It then goes on to show how Protestants, Catholics and Jews all agree with the Declaration's principles. (Notice that even Catholic monarchists agree that the King's authority derives from the consent of the governed.)

The second part of the chapter shows how the political tradition of the West, reaching back to pagan times, taught the same truths about the equality of men and the natural law as the Bible. It also mentions other aspects of that tradition that are pertinent to the later study of the Declaration and Constitution. The outline of the chapter should be very helpful here.

The idea of the "natural law" might present some difficulty for the student, and indeed for the teacher. Like much touched on in this chapter, entire books could be (and have been) written on the subject. However, it is important to distinguish the natural law from "laws of nature," like the laws of thermodynamics. These latter laws simply describe what must happen in nature, whether the subject wants them to or not. "Natural law" or the "law of nature" in a political sense, is the law that applies to all men because they share a common human nature. It is the only law that governs men who do not have a common society. It is distinguished from "positive law," which is law imposed by a particular government on a particular society.

Chapter Four — Thinking Through the Declaration

Outline of Chapter 4

- I. Independence, Revolution and Prudence [4.1]
  - A. Two duties
    1. Separation was a moral necessity or duty
    2. A duty to explain their actions to others

- B. Revolution
  1. Governments are to secure inalienable rights
     - a. Life, liberty and pursuit of happiness
     - b. Reasons for "pursuit of happiness" instead of "property"
  2. If government destroys these rights, the people may abolish it
     - a. They can replace old rulers (rebellion)
     - b. They can alter the form of government (revolution)
  3. Good government not only preserves rights, it aims at safety and happiness
- C. Prudence
  1. Prudence is thinking well about how to act
  2. The Declaration shows the Revolution was prudent

II. A Long Train of Abuses [4.2]

- A. The charges correspond to the branches of government, unjustly combined by the king
  1. The legislative
     - a. The charge is that the king has blocked good laws
     - b. The legislative power returns to the people
  2. The judicial
     - a. The king has failed to provide judges
     - b. The independence of the judges has been usurped
  3. The executive
     - a. Military policy
     - b. Excessive taxes and bureaucracy
     - c. Interference with the legislative and judicial powers
- B. The division of charges indicates the structure the Constitution will adopt

III. Words of power [4.3]

- A. The people declare themselves a separate nation
  1. Declarations are vows that make what they state come to be
  2. Separation was right; they submitted their decision to divine judgment
- B. Separation was worth the risk, because it is honorable to fight for liberty

When most people think of the Declaration of Independence, they recall the opening of the second paragraph: "We hold these truths..." They remember that the Declaration claimed that each individual has certain rights that have to be respected, and that we should fight to defend our rights. Unfortunately, since this is all most people remember about the Declaration, it often confirms in them a narrow, selfish, pugnacious stance in the face of real or perceived slights of their rights.

This chapter attempts in large part to broaden this narrow memory of the Declaration, by showing how it calls men in many ways above such a self-centered idea of rights. In one way, the text calls attention to the Declaration's use of such terms as "decent" and "sacred honor," that presuppose a noble view of the purposes and conduct of the political life. The student's attention should be drawn to these passages, as well as to the quotations found in the last of the Questions for Reflection (number 9). Although many in our society would take a cynical view of these phrases, considering them "smokescreens", they really show the political ideals of the founding generation.

A second way in which the Declaration combats the selfish view of rights is by its insistence on prudence. Even though the right to alter or abolish the government might exist, prudence demands that such a serious step only be taken when there are no other options, when rebellion becomes a duty, not just a right. Spend a little time discussing prudence with the students. Although not well thought of by many today, prudence, often called "practical wisdom," used to be considered one of the most important virtues. Prudence is a virtue of the mind that enables us to see what is the best thing to be done in the circumstance. It always keeps in mind the good to be achieved, and the circumstances that will help or hinder the attainment of the goal. Prudent men do not sacrifice principles, but they do look for ways in which their goals can be obtained without risking all. They also seek ways in which to defend their rights while accommodating the rights and needs of others.

In the colonists' case, they had to keep in mind the end they desired—a peaceful, free society—and determine the ways they could bring that about. Prudence also told them that no government would be perfect. So they had to be sure that they had tried all other avenues to attain freedom without war and revolution before they entered on the path of independence.

A third way in which the Declaration ennobles the desire for liberty is by claiming in various ways that government is a good. This is brought out in the text in the discussion of rights and ends. Government, although dangerous in many ways, is a necessary good because it secures the rights of all its citizens. Also, beyond the simple maintenance of rights, government has a role (undetermined in the document) in bringing about happiness. When we study the forms of government established by the new United States (chapter 5), we will see some of the ways in which these governments were enabled to promote the happiness of their citizens. The text also brings out how the list of charges against the king accuses him repeatedly of depriving the colonists of the benefits of good laws.

The second of the Questions for Reflection is very important for appreciating the wisdom and goodness of the American founding. Both the French and Russian Revolutions were undertaken to right extraordinary evils (worse than those the American colonists endured). The revolutionaries issued noble sounding declarations of human rights. You should have the students read the famous Declaration on Human Rights from the French Revolution. But both led to reigns of terror. Why? You should have the students investigate the view of religion taken by the governments formed from these revolutions. Also consider the following from Ambassador Alan Keyes, a black American orator of our times:

> "We fail to see, sometimes, that those great first principles of our nation's life... are not in the first instance a statement about rights. They are a statement about the authority from which those rights derive... And I will shamelessly stand on that Declaration... Because without it I believe that there is no protection in conscience from the inclinations and temptations of tyranny and oppression—no appeal, to any tribunal, once human beings have joined together, in their mobs, in order to oppress and destroy the rights of those so unfortunate as to fall under their power. You can try to convince me otherwise if you like, but I come from a background that will take a lot of convincing. My ancestors walked that dark path."

Chapter Five — American Constitutions

Outline for Chapter 5

- I. Introduction—Difficulties of forming a new government
  - A. Written constitutions had rarely been tried outside America
  - B. Even previous experience could not prevent many failures
- II. The Articles [5.1]
  - A. Confederation stronger than an alliance
    1. A united people
    2. A perpetual union
    3. States grant full privileges to other states' citizens
  - B. Limits of national government
    1. Most government tasks retained by states
    2. Given powers necessary to independent nations
  - C. Why the Articles failed

1. Inadequate power to act
2. Excessive difficulty of decision-making

III. The Preamble to the Constitution: goals of government [5.2]
   A. To establish a more perfect union
      1. Stronger powers
      2. Established by the people, not the states
   B. To establish justice through the rule of law
   C. To grant power to resist internal and external enemies
   D. To prevent sectionalism, but act for the good of the whole
   E. The blessings of liberty: beyond material goods and security

IV. The body of the Constitution [5.3]
   A. The Declaration is a guide to proper government.
   B. The people must be in charge: direct election
   C. The need for prudent deliberation
      1. Indirect election
      2. Separation of powers
      3. Measures to check sectionalism
   D. Safeguards of liberty

V. The Bill of Rights [5.4]
   A. Unnecessary and dangerous?
      1. Only the will of the people can defend liberty
      2. Explicit limitations imply powers that don't exist
   B. Limiting the national government: the 9th and 10th amendments
      1. The 10th: denies unlimited federal power
      2. The 9th: retains the rights of the people, which are prior to the Constitution
      3. Asking federal government to do too much erodes our liberty
   C. The Declaration helps interpret the Bill of Rights
      1. The First Amendment
         a. The role of religion in political life
         b. Not a complete "separation of church and state"
         c. Must not favor one sect over another
      2. The Second: the right of revolution demands armed citizens
      3. Bill of Rights and 'right' to abortion

In the Introduction to the textbook, the students saw abundant evidence to support the claim that our country was founded by the Declaration of Independence. In the strategies for that chapter, we mentioned that there are those who think our country was founded by the Constitution, not the

Declaration. This position leads to many dangerous errors, especially the view that our rights come from society rather than God.

In this chapter, we try to show how the two constitutions the U.S. has had in its history—the Articles and the Constitution—are properly understood, not as founding our country, but as instruments to make effective the commitment of the Declaration to form a united people under the laws of nature and nature's God. In the first section, we argue that the Articles of Confederation attempted to unite the people under a federal government; in the second section, we show how the Constitution fulfilled that end and made national self-government possible.

Important for understanding the role of the Articles of Confederation is grasping the significance of the word, "people". The Declaration speaks of the citizens of the colonies as one "people", and it is in the name of "the people" that the Congress dissolved political connections with Britain. Its use in the Declaration indicates that the formation of a people as one precedes their ability to form and give their consent to a government. The Declaration established the colonists as one people, even though it did not form the government that was to rule over the people.

The position of this book has been that the Declaration is America's founding creed, that it united the colonists into one people and stated the principles that were to guide the new society. Before the Declaration, the colonies were separate societies, but after it, they were one people. But a people needs a government. The Articles of Confederation were the first proposed form of government born of the Declaration. The fact the Articles were commissioned at the same time as the drafting of the Declaration gives great support to our earlier interpretation of the intention of the signers of the Declaration to form one people. However, the particular form of government does not make the people. This is why we date our country, legally and culturally, from 1776, even though the Constitution formed a radically different government from the Articles.

Besides this historical fact, the text of the Articles also confirms our interpretation of the intention of the Declaration. It is important that the students read over all the Articles referred to in the text that show this (XIII, IV, IX, and VI.) Some passages of the Articles are confusing, but the overall intent to form a government for one united people is clear. The intention to strengthen unity, and the perpetuity explicitly mentioned, will be important points in Abraham Lincoln's argument that the Southern states have no right to secede from the Union. From the Articles it is clear that Union is to be perpetual, even though the form of government may change.

The rest of the chapter is on the Constitution and has four major themes.

The first is found in the sub-section, "In Order to Form a More Perfect Union." The text here attempts to render intelligible to the student the passages from the Resolution of Congress and Washington's Letter of Transmittal. Questioning the students on the meaning of these passages will provide a good focus for discussion. They also reinforce the points from the previous section on the Articles, namely that the chief goal of both constitutions is making an effective government for a united people.

The second major theme is the idea that the goals stated in the Preamble are best understood in the light of the Declaration. The goals stated are important but very general and, consequently, vague. Our text is certainly not the last word on the subject. The exercises bring out some of the difficulties involved in the interpretation of the Preamble. A good question for discussion here might be: what do you do when a text is vague? As a statesman, should you act as though that leaves the door wide open for anything you might want to do, or are you safer to restrict its meaning and scope? Joseph Story's quotation is important for this discussion: the Preamble does not confer powers, but does tell for what purposes the powers granted in the Constitution are to be used.

The third main theme is that the body of the Constitution sets up structures and procedures that are a check on the people as much as on any one branch of government. It would be good to remind the students of the historical dangers of democracy mentioned back in chapter 1. These were very much on the founders' minds. It is also important to help the students see that these structures are not a denial of the freedom of the people. In our country, the people are still the rulers— "of the people, by the people and for the people." They are there to ensure that the people have the necessary time to cool off and think deliberately, so that their will when exercised is the most deliberate and most universally beneficial possible. It might be also good to point out that they could only make the national government so difficult to operate and change if they were presuming that most good and necessary things would be done by free associations or by lower levels of government. The more powerful the government, the more difficult it should be to operate and the more careful we should be that it only does what only it can do. Government should be limited in its scope.

The fourth theme is that the Declaration of Independence is especially helpful in understanding the Bill of Rights. Our times have been dominated by the disastrous effect of equating liberty with license. Misunderstandings of the Bill of Rights, to some extent sanctioned by the Supreme Court, have exacerbated what is always one of the biggest dangers for freedom-loving people. This final section first shows how the existence of a Bill of Rights invites an expansion of the federal authority, and second shows how key amendments need to be interpreted in a way that respects commitment to justice under God.

Chapter Six — The Stain of Slavery

Outline of Chapter 6

I. Introduction: does the Constitution condone slavery? [6]
  A. The language of the document shows aversion to slavery
  B. The words of the founders show that they consider slaves to be men
II. Declaration principles and early opposition to slavery [6.1]
  A. Attacks on slavery through preaching and legislation
  B. Congress banned slavery in the Northwest Territories
  C. Gradual abolition by the states before 1810
  D. Failure to complete the abolition
III. Prudence and principle at the Constitutional Convention [6.2]
  A. Southern adherence to slavery
  B. Danger of failure to form the Union
IV. Compromise and hope [6.3]
  A. Southerners ratify the Constitution
    1. Allowed a postponed ban on the slave trade
    2. Won 3/5 representation for their slaves
  B. Anti-slavery forces
    1. Constitution does not call slavery "legal"
    2. Abolition of slavery remains possible
  C. Reasons to hope for the end of slavery
V. Epilogue: How the hopes for an end of slavery died [6.3]
  A. Slaves increase in numbers and are used in more ways
  B. Some slaveholders begin to argue for it as good

Chapter 6 begins the second part of the course. In this half, we focus on what might be called "Declaration Statesmanship". Now that we have some understanding of the meaning of the Declaration and of how the Constitution embodies its principles, we turn to consider how those principles have been at work—or neglected—in some crucial periods of our history, and how they should inspire America and its leaders now. Chapter 6 shows how our founding fathers faced the tension between the principles of human dignity and the toleration of slavery, and how their efforts fell short of their goal.; chapter 7 looks at the Declaration Statesmanship of Abraham Lincoln with respect to this same question of slavery. Chapter 8 shows how the victory of the Civil War over slavery fell short of the Declaration ideal of political and social equality for all citizens, and how Martin Luther King, Jr., and others made further progress by appeal to that ideal. Chapter 9 together with the Epilogue looks at the contemporary crisis for Declaration principles, the crisis of American character.

The fifth of the Questions for Reflection contains a quotation that can set the stage for the whole chapter. Did the founders "put political expediency before the immorality of slavery"? Did they sacrifice principle for politics? The chapter's answer to this is complex, but finally it answers, "No." The founders were very careful to safeguard, even trumpet, the principle that "all men are created equal". Yet they were also firmly committed to the view that a united America was essential for the continued existence of the nation founded on that principle. Their Declaration Statesmanship consisted in saving the Union while ensuring that the principle of equality would be at work urging America to the ultimate elimination of slavery.

Helping students to understand and appreciate the statesmanship of the founders and of Lincoln will be difficult. Students are quick to suspect hypocrisy in politicians who seem to mouth principles but don't act according to them. Success will come from emphasizing 1) the necessity of union for the existence of America, 2) the importance of America's success as a republic for lovers of freedom around the world, and 3) the direct means that were taken to feed and strengthen the national repugnance over slavery.

With regard to the first two points, we strongly suggest that you review *Federalist 2, 6,* and *10*. With regard to the last point, two aspects should be noted. First, great care was taken by the founders to avoid a compromise of the principle while making compromises in policy: thus the use of "person" and avoidance of "slaves" in the Constitution, the refusal to use the word "legal" to describe slavery (the importance of language in expressing our actions cannot be overstated), and the insistence that the Constitution keep the federal government free to abolish the slave trade, to prohibit slavery's expansion into the territories, and even abolish it altogether. Second, there were many ways in which the nation inflamed and acted on its commitment to Declaration principles. For example, note Jefferson and Madison's vociferous attacks on slavery (see also Jefferson's first draft of the Declaration), the fervent religious condemnation of slavery at work forming American consciences, the outlawing of slavery in the Northwest Territories, and the abolishing of the slave trade in 1808.

The last section of chapter 6 sets the stage for the conflict discussed in chapter 7. As the slaveholders' financial interest in slavery increased, they and their southern neighbors rejected the Declaration view of it as a tolerated evil and began to embrace slavery as a foundational good, a "cornerstone". Madison's greatest fear for the Union was realized—a tremendous local faction had developed that denied the common basis of the good of all. The great question for American statesmanship in the middle of the 1800s became: Should we abandon the principles of the Declaration now that the Union's very existence is threatened?

Chapter Seven — The Politics of Abraham Lincoln

Outline For Chapter 7

I. Lincoln's early statesmanship: The speech to the Young Men's Lyceum [7.1]
   A. Lincoln saw a decline in adherence to Declaration principles
   B. His remedy: reason fortified by reverence for the laws
   C. Lincoln wanted to ennoble Americans' passion for their country
II. The House Divided [7.2]
   A. Missouri's admission delayed by slavery question
      1. South needed to prevent a Northern majority in the Senate
      2. North wanted to prevent expansion of slavery
   B. The Missouri Compromise
   C. South gets Mo. admitted as slave state
   D. North gets
      1. Line prohibiting slavery extended, most future states will come in free
      2. Congress's power to ban slavery in territories reaffirmed
      3. Rights of Negro citizens recognized
III. The compromise holds
   A. Six new states admitted, 3 slave and 3 free
   B. Compromise of 1850,
      1. California was admitted as a free state
      2. The North accepts a fugitive slave law
      3. Utah & N. Mex. free to decide on slavery when admitted
   C. Sectional bitterness over slavery worsened
      1. Pro-slavery apologists attacked the Declaration
      2. Abolitionists became more radical
      3. Fear of slave rebellion in South
      4. Hatred of fugitive slave law in North
   D. Douglas and "Popular Sovereignty"

1. Douglas supports the repeal of the Missouri Compromise
   a. Douglas was ambitious for presidency
   b. Wanted to preserve the Union by making a national debate over slavery unecessary
2. Proposed "Popular Sovereignty" as the American Principle
   a. This would end the discussion of whether slavery was wrong
   b. Makes principle of self-rule higher than natural law

IV. "Declaration Statesmanship" of the Peoria Speech (1854) [7.3]
   A. The equality of all men is a higher principle than majority rule
   B. Slavery in America is a disgrace to republican government everywhere
   C. Emancipation from slavery distinct from political & social equality
   D. Prudent statesmanship must respect the state of public opinion
   E. A return to the "ancient faith" of the Declaration
   F. Blending principle with charity

V. Supreme Court vs. the Declaration [7.4]
   A. Taney and the *Dred Scott* decision
      1. It denied Congress and the territories the right to prohibit slavery
      2. It also denied the equality of the races
      3. It attacked both principles: "Popular Sovereignty" and the Declaration's "all men created equal"
   B. Lincoln's response
      1. Submit to the decision in this case
      2. Work to have it overruled through political action
      3. Return the argument about slavery to the unifying principles of the Declaration

In chapter 7, we look at how statesmen imbued with Declaration principles have fought to keep this country on course to fulfill its commitment to honor the equal dignity of all men. We use the word, statesman, as distinct from politician. A politician is often primarily concerned with representing the interests of the particular groups that helped him get elected. A statesman, on the other hand, is one who, directed by an understanding of and reverence for the principles of a nation, acts to bring about the fundamental goods that touch all citizens. Every politician needs to exercise the virtues of a statesman in some measure; but many fail, and only a few rise to the kind of preeminence that enshrines them in hearts of their countrymen.

This chapter looks at Abraham Lincoln as the preeminent model of Declaration Statesmanship. In the face of challenges to the Declaration-based policy of the founders regarding slavery, Lincoln declared that he would offer his life to preserve the Union based on the principles of the Declaration. He succeeded in keeping America "one nation, under God, indivisible, with liberty and justice for all." The chapter shows some of the reasons for the success of his statesmanship: his unwavering commitment to Declaration principles, his wisdom in pursuing policies that would be principled yet acceptable to a majority of people, his ability to persuade, his courage in proclaiming the right, his charity towards his political enemies.

The first section shows Lincoln's early understanding of the political situation of his country. He recognized that in his lifetime America would need to build reverence for the law, for the principles of the Declaration, which would keep the people "attached to the government". Spend some time with the "Young Men's Lyceum" speech. You might open a discussion by having the students find passages which identify the three dangers mentioned in the outline of the speech, and any passages that suggest a remedy. Ask the students how many different kinds of men Lincoln considers in the speech, and what each of them might do in the face of a lawless society. Have selected students take sections of the speech and read them aloud. Encourage them to prepare by raising questions where they don't understand the point, then read them dramatically. (This last suggestion can be applied to any of the quotations in the chapter.)

The next part of the chapter reviews the two main legislative compromises regarding slavery. The student should already be familiar with the history; you might have to refresh the students on some of the details. Our review is intended to point out the consistency of these compromises with principle: a national commitment to the limitation and gradual extinction of slavery. Use the outline to point out the chief ways in which these compromises kept the policy intact. You might ask whether the 1850 Compromise shows any signs of weakening.

The third section shows how Lincoln responded to attacks on the Declaration-based policy on slavery, first by Douglas, then by the *Dred Scott* decision. Discuss how Douglas' "Popular Sovereignty" doctrine is a "repudiation of the old faith" of the founders. Discuss how *Dred Scott* undercut both Douglas and Lincoln, and how they both responded to it. Lincoln's commitment to Declaration principles and to reverence for the rule of law was severely tried by the Supreme Court. Did he find a policy that allowed him to be faithful to both?

Chapter Eight — Jim Crow and the Civil Rights Movement

Outline for Chapter 8

I. Reconstruction [8.1]
   A. Southern Reconstruction
      1. What should be done for the recently freed slaves?
      2. The Dem. President & Dem. Southern governments:
         a. Enacted "Black Codes" restricting freedom of blacks
         b. Refused voting rights
         c. Tolerated violence against the freed men
   B. Northern reaction (Radical Reconstruction)
      1. Congress passed Fourteenth and Fifteenth Amendments
      2. Established military governors over South
      3. "Carpetbaggers" & the corruption of new coalition governments
   C. Southern back-lash: violence and the Ku Klux Klan
   D. Northern weariness & withdrawal of support for equal treatment

II. "Jim Crow" [8.2]
   A. For twenty years, the freedmen exercised their rights
   B. In 1890s, Populists turn against black labor and white leaders
      1. United around goals of segregation & disenfranchisement
         a. Racism in the West
         b. Lynchings in Midwest and South
      2. Mob rule across nation
   C. "Jim Crow" laws enact segregation and voter discrimination

III. The Civil Rights Movement and the Declaration [8.3]
   A. Overview
      1. Segregation was unchecked for 60 years
      2. Jim Crow eventually defeated by religious, moral, and Declaration principles
   B. The Supreme Court and segregation
      1. Harlan's dissent in *Plessy v. Ferguson*: the Constitution is colorblind
      2. *Brown v. Board of Education* struck down segregation due to its effects, not principle
      3. Court still allows race as a factor in affirmative action laws
   C. Choices facing men of faith in the face of injustice
      1. The Martyr: set an example of virtue and pray
      2. The Knight: fight for justice in God's name

D. Exemplars of the struggle for full equality
   1. Booker T. Washington: The Martyr
   2. W.E.B. Du Bois: The Knight of Civil Rights
E. Martin Luther King, Jr: The Declaration Statesman
   1. Faced with a failure to apply founding principles to all Americans
   2. As a citizen-statesman, his tools were protests and lawsuits
      a. Need to energize the resistence to Jim Crow
      b. Desire to win hearts and minds and to unify
   3. A new approach: non-violent protest
      a. The courage of Du Bois and the charity of Washington
      b. The law as a moral instructor

Chapter 8 highlights the failures in Declaration Statesmanship on the question of racial equality that occurred from Lincoln's death until the rise of another Declaration statesman, Martin Luther King, Jr.

The first section of this part sets the stage for understanding the crisis. The Southern states after the Civil War and the northern Radical Reconstructionists abandoned the wisdom of Lincoln's Declaration policies. The Southerners chose to deny freed blacks the equality under the law which was due to them; the Northerners, without their prudent head, Lincoln, reacted vindictively and so ultimately failed to bring about their desired goal—the full implementation of the Fourteenth and Fifteenth Amendments. You might want to engage your students on the question of the Reconstructionist policy, comparing their pure policies with the more limited, more prudent policies of the founding fathers and Lincoln. Lincoln ensured that the North remained committed to the principles that would end slavery, while the Reconstructionists ultimately lost the moral support of the North as well as the South, and abandoned the blacks to their segregated fate. McKinley's policy of abandoning principle for public quiet contrasts strikingly with Lincoln's.

In the second section, Martin Luther King, Jr., is shown to return to Lincoln's policy of manfully keeping principle before the eyes of the American people, moving them to a proper, determined and lasting response to evil.

Chapter Nine — A People Worthy of the Declaration

Outline For Chapter 9

I. The character of our forefathers [9.1]

   A. Tocqueville found America's success to be founded on character and customs
   B. Early Americans' experience in self-government
      1. Independent property owners
      2. Voluntary associations
      3. Individualism
II. Requirements for a free people [9.2]
   A. Taking responsibility
   B. Prudence: making good decisions
   C. Willingness to participate in civic life
III. Forming free citizens [9.3]
   A. Religious formation
      1. Benefits of prohibiting establishment of religion
      2. Religion as a restraint on abuse of power
      3. Religion as encouragement of trust and security
   B. Educational formation
      1. Liberal education and principles of natural law
      2. Knowledge of rights and government
      3. Encouraging morality, sobriety, and enterprise

This course, like all civics courses, has a very practical aim—to give students who are our future citizens insight into the principles of our American Republic, in the hope that they will come to love them. This chapter aims to encourage students to apply those principles in their own lives in the face of the many particular challenges of our times. As Hamilton, Tocqueville and Lincoln understood, our country always has been and always will be an experiment. With over three centuries of successful democratic government, it is easy to fool ourselves into thinking our way of life is forever secure, but it is not. Any government that depends upon the virtue of the citizens is only as reliable as its citizens. You can hardly overemphasize the need for each generation to commit itself anew to the ideals we have been treating.

The chapter first looks at the customs that Tocqueville thought made America successful as a democracy. Experience in property ownership and in self-government; a healthy sense of individualism tempered by the vigorous employment of non-governmental associations; a general education that equipped them to govern; and widespread piety.

The second section invites students to consider the relationship of the life of a free man to responsibility, civic duty, education, self-control and religious worship.

We have emphasized the need for prudence in the virtuous life. As Aristotle pointed out, virtue generally lies between two extremes. It also has many different manifestations depending on varying circumstances. The reflections in this chapter should be considered to be the opportunities for discussion with and between students. For this reason there are no review questions in this chapter.

Epilogue

Outline of Epilogue

I. A new notion of freedom
   A. The old ideal and its power to reform
   B. Freedom equals license
   C. Denying free choice
II. Attacks on the family
   A. Family is the training ground for morality
   B. Homosexual "marriage"
   C. Judicial usurpation
III. Education aimed at getting a job
   A. Relativism & multiculturalism cause moral uncertainty
   B. Planned job placement at odds with innovation and growth
   C. Loss in confidence that reason can guide judgment
IV. Attacks on religion
   A. Keeping religion out of education
   B. Keeping religion out of politics
   C. Resulting materialism and license
V. Living the Declaration

This final section points out contemporary cultural trends that threaten to make the free life impossible. There are no review questions, and the students are not tested on the content of the Epilogue in the final exam.

Comments on the Questions for Reflection

Note regarding these comments:

Much of what is provided here is factual information for the convenience of a busy teacher. We hope that the Questions for Reflection *will* provoke reflection and discussion, and they do not all have 'answers'. There are a number of deep or controversial questions raised in our book, and decent and informed people may well answer some of them differently. These remarks to the teacher are meant to provide guidance for those who feel in need of it; the opinions expressed in them are not meant to be dogmatic or authoritative.

Introduction Questions for Reflection:

1. The pyramid has the year 1776 inscribed on the base, indicating that year as the beginning of the United States. (The commission to design a Great Seal for the new country was made at almost the same time as the commission to draft Articles of Confederation in 1776.)

   The original committee consisted of Benjamin Franklin, Thomas Jefferson, and John Adams, but none of the designs they submitted was accepted. A second committee was formed in 1780, and a third in 1782. That year the Secretary of Congress, Charles Thomson, took elements from the work of all three committees and submitted a written description, which was accepted June 20, 1782. It is interesting that one of the earliest designs by Franklin showed Moses leading Israel through the Red Sea, which is the event that forged the unity of Israel as a nation not merely tribal but united by a law. Common to all the designs was the motto *e pluribus unum.*

   The Great Seal is used on documents such as military insignia, treaties, commissions, and passports, and it is displayed on the gates of embassies. All these signify the acts of a sovereign nation in a community of other nations.

   Other things to notice:

   - The phrase *anuit coeptus* is from the first line of Virgil's *Aeneid.* The "he" who favors the undertaking is Jove in the original context. Here it indicates that God has favored the new nation.
   - The phrase *novus ordo saeclorum,* also taken (somewhat freely) from Virgil, suggests a transforming moment in history. Dante and many

others in the Middle Ages thought Virgil (who is Dante's guide in *The Divine Comedy*) had prophetic knowledge of the Christian era.
- "Out of many, one" indicates unity, and the rows of stone in the pyramid, the arrows in the eagles claw and the laurel leaves in his other claw all number 13, for the 13 colonies.
- The olive branch and arrows both held by one eagle show unity in peace and war.
- The eye is a commonly used symbol for the all-seeing eye of God. (It is used thus by the Masons, but was not invented by them, and there is no need to assume a secret Masonic influence to account for its presence here.)

2. Preceding the signatures at the end of the Constitution is a sentence referring to 1787 as the twelfth year of independence. "A more perfect union" implies a previously existing imperfect union.
3. The universal consensus is that the country started in 1776. It would be hard to tell what year is the proper bicentennial of the Constitution: the year it was submitted to the states for ratification? The year it was ratified by 9 states and so became effective in those states? The year the 13th and final state ratified? But with the Declaration it is different. To declare independence is to effect independence: the Declaration is words of power, like the marriage vows.

Chapter 1 Questions for Reflection:

1. If you wish to give this research assignment to your student(s) there is nothing wrong with starting with Wikipedia. Another good place to start for persons and events leading up to and during the American Revolution is Samuel Eliot Morison's book, *Oxford History of the American People.* It is always good to find more than one source.
2. (no comment)
3. (no comment)

Chapter 2 Questions for Reflection:

1. Sample Outline of Declaration
   a) Introduction (paragraph 1)
   b) The argument that the colonies must separate from Britain (pars. 2–20)
      i. What in general makes rebellion necessary (pars. 2–4)

ii. Application of the general principles to the situation of the colonies (pars. 5–23)
   A. The king is charged with attempting to establish absolute tyranny
   B. 18 specific accusations supporting the general charge
iii. Conclusion (pars. 24–26)
   A. The king is a tyrant
   B. The British people have not listened to our pleas

c) The declaration of independence (pars. 27–32)

2. (no comment)
3. God is referred to four times, under the titles of "Nature's God" (par. 1), "Creator" (par. 2), "Supreme Judge of the World" (par. 27), and "Divine Providence" (par. 32).
4. Charges 1–7 correspond to government's legislative function; charges 8–9 correspond to its judicial function; the remainder correspond to its executive function. See also the answer to Question for Reflection 3 in chapter 5.
5. (no comment)
6. (no comment)

Chapter 4 Questions for Reflection:

1. These texts seem to command submission even to unjust or oppressive rulers.
2. for the doctrine that all men are created equal:

   "God has provided a Rule . . . obliging each one to the performance of that which is right. . . " (Wise)

   "The Third Capital Immunity . . . is an equality amongst Men. . . " (Wise)

   "in a state of nature men are equal. . . " (Hitchcock)

   that they are endowed with certain inalienable rights:

   "The Second Great Immunity of Man is an Original Liberty. . . " (Wise)

   ". . . the people. . . have not only a right, but are bound in duty, for the preservation of the property and liberty of the whole society. . . " (Hitchcock)

   "There are several things which he may not give away,. . . Others which he ought not. . . " (Witherspoon)

   that the source of the just powers of government derive from the consent of the governed:

"...no Sovereignty can be Established, unless some Human Deed or Covenant Precede..." (Wise)

"The first Human Subject and Original of Civil Power is the People." (Wise)

"...magistrates have no authority but what they derive from the people..." (West)

"[political power's] origin is from the people..." (Hitchcock)

3. (no comment)
4. One of the challenges this course presents to the teacher is that it intends to stretch the student's vocabulary and reading muscles. We have not dumbed things down, and we ask student and teacher alike to grapple with sometimes difficult language. It is our hope that the students will be better writers and readers after completing the course.
5. A fine author on this question is C.S. Lewis in *Mere Christianity* and *The Abolition of Man.* A prominent public thinker in our times is Robert P. George of Princeton, whose writings are available on the internet.
6. Yes, there are virtues connected to the acquisition and protection of property. We're thinking of something like this: Do you endeavor to teach your children thrift? Is saving money a moral virtue?
7. Equal as members of the human species which is defined by freedom and reason. Equal in dignity as self-governing rational creatures.
8. (no comment)
9. There are too many examples to list here. New York State alone has Athens, Attica, Babylon, Brutus, Cairo, Canaan, Carthage, Cicero, Cincinnatus, Corinth, Greece, Hector, Homer, Ilion, Ithaca, Lysander, Macedon, Malta, Manlius, Marathon, Marcellus, Minerva, Ovid, Palmyra, Phoenicia, Rome, Romulus, Sardinia, Scio, Scipio Center, Syracuse, Troy, Utica, Vestal, and West Seneca. Georgia has a Rome, an Athens, an Augusta and a Homer.

   There are names honoring contemporary English monarchs and nobility, such as Maryland (Queen Mary, wife of King Charles I), the Carolinas (King Charles), Georgia (King George), Baltimore (Lord Baltimore) and Charlottesville (Queen Charlotte, wife of King George III), New York (Duke of York). An exception to the rule against honoring ancient monarchs would seem to be Alexandria, VA, which might make one think of Alexander the Great, but it was actually named for a Scotsman, John Alexander, who purchased the land in 1669.
10. (no comment)
11. (no comment)

12. The Whig Party was on the whole pro-Parliament and (mildly) opposed to kings and nobles, in contrast to the Tory Party.

    It also had a strong Protestant (William and Mary) vs. Catholic (King Charles) overtone. It was regarded positively in America. Some prominent Whigs (Pitt, Burke) favored the American cause.

    The English Bill of Rights comes out of the Glorious Revolution, as does the establishment of the Anglican Church as the official state religion.

Chapter 4 Questions for Reflection:

1.
    - happiness: good fortune or blessedness
    - denounce: announce (not 'criticize')
    - bands: ties, connections
    - prudence: practical wisdom, good judgment (not primarily caution)
    - assume: take on
    - endowed: gifted
    - unalienable: incapable of being separated from
    - ends: goals
    - transient: fleeting, short-lived
    - light: insignificant, opposite of 'weighty'
    - usurpations: unjust or illegal takings
    - evinces: shows (related to the word 'evidence')
    - despotism: tyranny
    - people: united body of persons
2. The Russian and, to a lesser extent, the French Revolutions aimed at overturning a whole order of life. The American, in contrast, aimed to a large extent at preserving many of the goods the colonists had enjoyed under the English kings. Religious life went on in America after the revolution just as it had before, whereas religion was persecuted and oppressed under the French and Russian revolutionary regimes. Both the French and the Russians destroyed the very individuals who started them and the free government they attempted to set up. But George Washington became President lawfully and peacefully, retired voluntarily from public life, and died peacefully in his bed.
3. Some examples of historical events referred to in the charges:
    - Charge 5 might refer to the dissolutions, by royal governors, of the assembly of Massachusetts and of the House of Burgesses in Virginia (1774), also New York's Assembly (1768).

- Charge 7 may refer in part to the establishment by King George of an "Indian Preserve" in the mountains west of the settled land.
- Charge 9 may refer to provisions of the Townshend Acts (1767) to shift payment of the salaries of royal governors and judges to the crown.
- Charge 11 refers to the British military presence beginning in 1764.
- Charge 13 refers to the king's support of the pretensions of Parliament (the "jurisdiction foreign to our consitution") to legislate for the colonies.
- Charge 14 refers to the Quartering Act of 1765.
- Charge 15 refers to incidents such as the burning of Falmouth, Maine, and the destruction of the town of Norfolk, Virginia in 1775.
- Charge 20 refers to an attempt the king made, in order to conciliate the French Catholics in Quebec, to replace the English Common Law system there with the French legal system based on Roman law.
- Charge 26 refers to British attempts to recover sailors who had deserted from the British Navy and were working on American ships; when they stopped an American ship looking for these deserters, they were not very scrupulous about identification, and likely to seize any sailor that appeared to be British.
- Charge 27 plays on the fears of those along the western frontiers of Indian attacks; there had been 'massacres' (of both Indians and settlers), and there was the memory of a bitterly fought war with Indians in New England ("King Philip's War"); in the French and Indian War, both the French and the British had enlisted Indian allies and some of the tribes still had ties to the British king. (See also the comment on question 5 below.)

4. If the charges are overstated, it diminishes the reputation of those making the charges, but does not necessarily impugn the rightness and solidity of the government structures they erected.
5. There were attempts to stir up slaves in Virginia to flee from their masters and aid the British in exchange for their freedom. It was widely feared that this would lead to widespread and destructive slave insurrections. Again we see that there was a tension, almost a contradiction, between the fact of slavery and the principles of the Declaration. The working out of this tension becomes one of the principal features of our history.
6.
    - impartial judges, not subject to influence from other branches
    - lean and efficient government (contrasted to the "swarm" of officials)
    - privacy in homes and respect for private property

- local legislatures
- protection from outside dangers, and domestic subjection of the military to civil power
- protection and encouragement of international trade
- trial by jury
- transparent and effective legislative control over taxation

These are still aims of the American government. It is manifest that in our current political arguments some hold fast to Declaration principals and others appear to be directly opposing them. It is also true that the application of these principles is not always clear. Think of arguments about domestic security vs. privacy rights (NSA, drones, monitoring of phone records), national security vs. supremacy of the civil government (Vietnam, Iraq, Afghanistan). Consider also the conflict between the good of an impartial and independent judiciary and the danger of that becoming an independent and usurping judiciary (abortion, gay marriage).

7. The right to revolt is restricted by a higher law, and it was precisely that understanding that made the Congress believe they had to give reasons, "submit facts to a candid world", as part of their declaration. This higher law comes from the Supreme Judge of the world. The possibility of just rebellion against the new government is indeed presumed by the principles of the Declaration, but only on the conditions set forth in the Declaration, i.e., a long train of abuses, destructive of the secure enjoyment of life, liberty, and the pursuit of happiness. Because this possibility always exists, we must work constantly to sustain our liberty —"Eternal vigilance is the price of Liberty."
8. The thoughtless denigration of the political life as inevitably corrupt and futile, a smug sense that politicians are to be despised with no corresponding effort to improve things, pervasive and comfortable cynicism; all these things discourage noble minds from pursuing politics as a career.
9. (no comment)

Chapter 5 Questions for Reflection:

1. The readings recommended explain at greater length how the constitution intended to consolidate the Union and give the federal government effectual powers over both citizens and the states so as to realize the ends of that Union. They give many particular instances of the inability of Congress to govern under the Articles.

2. Article I, section 8, especially subsections 1, 2, and 18. Also, from the Preamble, "promote the general welfare." *Alexander Hamilton*, by Ron Chernow, is a good source for this and the following question.
3. This is perhaps an open question. If you ask your students to think about it, you might ask them to list both pros and cons.
4. The verbs are:
   - form
   - establish
   - insure
   - provide for
   - promote
   - secure
   - ordain
   - establish

   Urge your students to look up these words in a good dictionary and see what you find. Here are some examples:
   - form a more perfect union equals 'shape up' the Union so that it is 'more complete.'
   - Establish equals 'set up and make firm.'
   - Insure equals 'make secure' (think 'insurance').
   - Provide, from the Latin: *pro* plus *video*, equals look ahead, foresee. Consider that the military has plans for future dangers and must have resources on hand before any danger becomes real.
   - Promote (*pro* and motion) equals move forward. The Constitution looks to economic growth and greater and greater prosperity.
   - Secure equals 'obtain and make safe.'
   - Ordain equals 'commands to be by genuine authority.' Here the power rests in the people. Compare to 'ordain a minister' or priest, 'commission an officer.'
5. In case it is not clear from this question itself, the difference of opinion about state sovereignty will lie at the bottom of the difference of opinion about a "right of secession". Is the Union entirely a compact between sovereign states or is it a solemn act of "we the People"?

   Note that the ratification called for in Article VII, though carried out state by state, is not an act of the state governments, but of the people of each state, meeting in a convention outside the governmental structure of the state.

   The Union side of this controversy is powerfully argued by President Lincoln in his July 1861 "Message to Congress."
6. Limitations on the power of the national government can be found in:

- Article I, Section 3, subsection 6
- Article I, Section 9
- Article III, Sections 2 and 3
- Article IV, Section 2, subsection 3
- Article V
- Article VI, Section 3

7. There was no power to tax individuals; revenues could only be raised from the states. There was no separate executive branch, and essentially no separate judiciary branch. There was no 'supremacy' clause (see Article VI, Section 2 of the Constitution). A review of the list of grievances in the Declaration will show how many more are not about bad law, but absence of law.
8. Review the Constitution, or the textbook, on the first part of the question. For the second part, one may simply say that the Declaration claims that King George had united all the branches of government into one in his person.
9. This is a deep question. A minimal answer is that a republican form of government is one in which all power is derived directly or indirectly from the people. It seems right to add to this the principle of representation (instead of all citizens voting directly on every decision) and the rule of law (which restricts what the government can do, even with a majority vote). The most simple democracy could lack both of these things. Classic texts for this question are *Federalist 14* and *39*. It seems to us that Article IV, Section 4, does indeed limit state sovereignty.
10. As to the historical question, nearly all the states had established religions through the founding period. Only Pennsylvania and Rhode Island had laws guaranteeing religious toleration. We will return to this question in chapter 9 when we discuss the First Amendment.
11. (no comment)
12. (no comment)

Chapter 6 Questions for Reflection:

1. Simon Bolivar, the great liberator of South America from Spanish rule, tried in vain to unite the colonies. Bolivar was the first president of Gran Columbia (the northwest part of the continent, including Venezuela, Ecuador and northern Peru), but the federation was weak, and broke apart after ten years (1819–1830). During its brief and troubled existence, there were territorial border wars with the southern part of Peru (1828 and 1829).

The Federal Republic of Central America was not strong enough to defend itself against the First Empire of Mexico, which occupied it.

The United Provinces of South America (including southern Peru, Chile, and Argentina) went to war with Brazil in the 1820s over the territory which became independent Uruguay as a result.

From 1836–1839 the newly formed Peru-Bolivian Confederation was at war with Chile and Argentina, fighting over control of commercial routes in the Pacific.

The Uruguayan Civil War of 1838–1851 involved the neighboring nations of Brazil and the Argentine Confederacy.

In the 1860s, Peru and Chile were at war with Spain, disputing control of guano-rich islands off the coast, and from 1879 to 1883 they were again fighting each other over control of mineral-rich provinces.

Meanwhile in the east, Paraguay was fighting the Triple Alliance of Argentina, Brazil, and Uruguay, in a war whose causes are still disputed, but which resulted in the highest rate of fatalities relative to combatants of any war in modern history.

2. The moral question of slavery was identical for North and South. The social and economic aspects already impacted the South much more than the North, and this difference would only increase as the plantation system spread and flourished. Plantation agriculture was well established in the South by 1787. The Southern economy was agriculture based, and the customary way of making the land productive on large properties in the South already involved large numbers of slaves. In the North, agricultural production was more typically from small properties, while Northern industry and commerce, a significant and growing portion of the economy, was almost entirely independent of slavery.
3. It seems probable. Factors to consider are: 1.) climate and farmland suitable for large-scale agriculture, 2.) new settlers attracted to this fertile and open land, many of them bringing slaves with them, 3.) race-prejudice, which relegated African Americans to servile labor, 4.) the opposition to slavery by settlers from New England on religious/moral grounds (the southern portions of this territory however would also attract settlers from the neighboring slave states of Kentucky and Virginia—remember: West Virginia is still part of Virginia), 5.) the legal difficulties of out-lawing slavery when there was no bar to slave-owners entering the territory with their "property."
4. a) Life, because although the slave-owner did not have the legal right of life and death over his slave, the legal protections that existed were inadequate in law and impotent in practice. b) Liberty, of course. c) Pursuit of

happiness, of course. You might think about why it would later be so important for those justifying slavery to claim that the slaves were happy. The image of the singing, dancing, carefree slave became a standard stereotype.

Your students may assume that abolition of slavery is identical with the granting of equal civil rights, and it is important that they are aware of the distinction between these two goals.

5. Prudence and idealism are not always congruent, but true prudence always looks toward the ideal. The statesman must of course acknowledge the reality of the past and the present, but, especially where it falls short of the good, the true and the just he must, by word and deed, show a path toward what is truly right. A revolution which attempts to wipe the slate clean and start anew is doomed to failure. Compare the heart-breaking French and Russian experiences of revolution to our own.
6. The passages relevant to slavery in the Constitution are (a) the fugitive slave clause (Article 4, Section 2, Clause 3) (b) the three-fifths rule (Article 1, Section 2, Paragraph 3), and (c) the limit on the slave trade (Article 1, Section 9, Clause 1). The Constitution, by avoiding the use of the word, never admits the existence of a category or race of men born to be slaves.
7. (no comment)
8. (no comment)
9. (no comment)

Chapter 7 Questions for Reflection:

1. Re-read carefully the last paragraph of the Lyceum Speech.
2. "Faithfully." Two meanings come to mind: A thing can be expressed faithfully in reference to the concept—the words are faithful to the idea. But it may also refer to faith in the teachings of God. Coolidge, who thought that American principles derived from Christianity, may be referring to the latter.
3. This is meant to be a challenging question to your students. Are your students familiar with G.K. Chesterton's wonderful expression, "the democracy of the dead"? From his book *Orthodoxy*: "Tradition means giving votes to the most obscure of all classes, our ancestors. It is the democracy of the dead. Tradition refuses to submit to the small and arrogant oligarchy of those who merely happen to be walking about."
4. The love of comforts tempts men to become lax in performing their political duties. The resulting descent into tyranny is thus self-induced.

There is always a potential tyrant among us, looking to take advantage of an opportunity.

5. (no comment needed)
6. (no comment needed)
7. Perhaps the president could refuse to enforce the Court's decision beyond the immediate case, that is, not allow it to be used as a binding "precedent" for future cases. Consider the prudence or imprudence of such a course.
8. This is a speculative question to which we do not propose any answer.
9. (no comment needed)

Comments on Chapter 8 Questions for Reflection:

1. This issue is part of the current discussion of citizenship for illegal immigrants. It will surprise many that is, in fact, still possible to serve in our army without citizenship: should such soldiers be granted citizenship after their service?
2. (no comment needed)
3. (no comment needed)

Chapter 9 Questions for Reflection:

1. (no comment needed)
2. A farmer owning his own property, compared to a tenant farmer, will reasonably have more care for the preservation of the land. A child in a family who owns a bicycle, or a dog, and is given the responsibility of caring for it is another example.
3. (no comment needed)
4. Men have a hard time living by reason alone. To believe in God in some way appears to be both natural and helpful in living a good life.
5. Both churches and public schools, particularly in New England, were energetic in promoting literacy. The place to look in the Northwest Ordinance is Section 14, Article 3.
6. (no comment needed)
7. Federal grants and loans, the G.I. Bill after WWII, and similar federal assistance, have enabled students to attend private religious colleges. On the one hand, the country's reasonable goal of encouraging education at all levels would justify helping students to attend any college. On the other hand, once such funding has been accepted, the threat of its withdrawal gives the government an unwarranted power to influence

admissions, hiring, and even curriculum. This has been the case in regard to affirmative action.

8. (no comment)

Chapter Review Answers

Chapter 1 Review Questions

1. Put the following events in order; write the date (year, month if possible) for each. (Remember, this is not a history book; a little research on your part is necessary from time to time.)
   a) Continental Congress approves Declaration of Independence
   b) British government first imposes taxes on American colonies
   c) Continental Congress declares independence
   d) British parliament declares right to make laws for American colonies
   e) Battles of Lexington and Concord
   f) Coercive Acts (Intolerable Acts)
   g) Falmouth, Maine, burned
   h) Boston Tea Party
   i) First Continental Congress meets
   j) Boston Massacre
   k) Olive Branch Petition

   ANSWERS

   b. *British government first imposes taxes on American colonies (March 1765)*
   d. *British parliament declares right to make laws for American colonies (March 1766)*
   j. *Boston Massacre (March 1770)*
   h. *Boston Tea Party (December 1773)*
   f. *Coercive Acts (Intolerable Acts) (Spring 1774)*
   i. *First Continental Congress meets (September 1774)*
   e. *Battles of Lexington and Concord (April 1775)*
   k. *Olive Branch Petition (July 1775)*
   g. *Falmouth, Maine, burned (October 1775)*
   c. *Continental Congress declares independence (July 2, 1776)*
   a. *Continental Congress approves Declaration of Independence (July 4, 1776)*

   Notes to the teacher:

   There was a Sugar Tax in 1764, which preceded the more well-known Stamp Tax of 1765. But the act was actually a reduction in a tax from 1733, accompanied with a serious enforcement of it.

   The dissolving of the Massachusetts Legislature was done by the royal governor, based on provisions of the Coercive Acts, which were not in themselves intended to deny self-government.

Falmouth was in Massachusetts at the time (Maine was not yet a state.) The site is now the town of Portland, Maine (not Falmouth, Massachusetts, nor Falmouth, Maine!)

2. What three authorities did the American colonists cite as ntitling them "to life, liberty, and property"? *The immutable laws of nature, the principles of the English Constitution, and the several charters or compacts.* (page 9)
3. Name three ways in which Parliament asserted its right to make laws for the colonies.
   a) *Acts of 1764, including taxation, search and seizure, and providing for the British troops in the colonies;*
   b) *Declaration of 1766;*
   c) *the Coercive Acts of 1774, including the suspension of the Massachusetts' legislature.*
4. We note five facts that indicate differences between the principles of Athenian democracy and our own. The following statements from famous American documents show the contrast. Match each quotation below with one of the points (beginning on page 13).
   a) "From the disorders that disfigure the annals of those [Greek and Italian] republics the advocates of despotism have drawn arguments, not only against the forms of republican government, but against the very principles of civil liberty."—*Federalist 9*

      (5) The power and glory of the Athenians...
   b) "[Governments derive] their just powers from the consent of the governed." —Declaration of Independence *(3) Athens acquired an empire...*
   c) "Congress shall make no law respecting an establishment of religion nor prohibiting the free exercise thereof, or abridging the freedom of speech."— The Constitution of the United States

      (1) The same Athenian democracy that reared Socrates...
   d) "All men are created equal [and are] endowed by their Creator with certain unalienable rights." —Declaration of Independence

      (4) Pericles himself calls democracy...
   e) "That among these are life, liberty and the pursuit of happiness." —Declaration of Independence

      (2) The wealth and culture of the city...
5. What was Parliament? Name two duties that Parliament exercised under the king.

   Parliament was a council of nobles, clergy, and representatives of important towns that (1)advised the king on legislative matters; (2)the king needed the agreement of Parliament to impose new taxes.

6. How did the "Glorious Revolution" of 1688 lead to difficulties between Britain and the American colonies?

   The Glorious Revolution made Parliament a superior authority to the king; Parliament later tried to extend its authority over the colonies that were subject to the king.
7. Write a brief quotation from Thomas Paine's *Common Sense* that argues that:
   a) monarchy is not supported by the Bible
   b) monarchy is inimical to liberty.

   a) *"Government by Kings was first introduced into the world by the heathens, from whom the children of Israel copied the custom."*
   b) *"A thirst for Absolute power is the natural disease of monarchy."*
8. Fill in the blanks:
   a) In Athens, democracy was based on *power*; American colonists thought that democracy should be based on *the law of nature, the equality of all men, or justice.*
   b) Two sources that taught Americans about the laws of nature were *political philosophers like John Locke* and *the Bible.*

Chapter 2 Review Questions

No chapter review questions

Chapter 3 Review Questions

1. On page 35, the text says, "...the Bible claims that [the Declaration's self-evident truths] are known by reason as well as by faith." What does "known by reason" mean?

   That all men can know them naturally, without any special revelation from God.
2. What is meant by "natural law" or the "law of nature"?

   The reasonable plan for human life, by which we know our rights and duties that follow from our common humanity. (page 36)
3. What is the difference between a right and a duty?

   A right is a claim we have to keep something we have or receive something someone else owes us; a duty is an obligation we owe to others.

4. What are the three "great immunities" identified by John Wise?
   Man is the proper subject of the Law of Nature; Liberty; and Equality. (page 37)
5. What reason does Wise give to support his claim that "no Sovereignty can be Established, unless some Human Deed, or Covenant Precede?"
   All men are born free; nature has made them equal. (page 38)
6. Samuel West says, "... [t]he authority of a tyrant is null and void." What two statements does he make to argue for this claim?
   a) *"No man can have a right to act contrary to the law of nature"*
   b) *"No individual, or even a great number of men, can confer a right upon another of which they themselves are not possessed."* (page 38)
7. How does John Witherspoon distinguish alienable from unalienable rights?
   Alienable rights can be surrendered or given up; unalienable rights cannot be surrendered. (page 39)
8. What does Aristotle identify as man's specific difference?
   Man is the animal that thinks, the rational animal. (page 40)
9. What does Aristotle mean by defining man as a "social or political animal"?
   He lives best in society with other men. (page 44)
10. What did Aristotle consider the best achievable form of political organization?
    A polity or constitutional government in which the majority, men of ordinary means, and the owners of large property check each other. (page 44)
11. Who is the truly happy man according to Aristotle?
    The person who lives according to reason and the moral virtues, with a suitable share of this world's goods. (page 45)
12. Identify two doctrines that Jefferson might have learned from Cicero.
    There is a higher law that all governments must obey, and all men are equal under natural law. (page 45)
13. What is the definition of political power according to Locke? What is its purpose?
    Political power is a "right of making laws with penalties of death, and consequently all lesser penalties." Its purpose is the regulation and preservation of property. (page 46)
14. According to Locke, how are political communities formed? Why are they formed in this way?
    They are formed by consent, that is by each man "agreeing with other men to join and unite into a community." They are formed this way because "men are by nature free, equal, and independent." (page 48)

15. Name three Declaration principles David Hume found in the writing of Algernon Sydney.

    the original contract

    the source of power in the consent of the people

    the lawfulness of resisting tyrants

    ("The preference of liberty to the government of a single person" is not mentioned in the Declaration.)

Chapter 4 Review Questions

1. What does the Declaration mean by calling separation from Britain a "necessity?"

    It means that separation from Britain is a duty, that is, a moral necessity. (page 57)
2. According to the Declaration, why do we have unalienable rights to life, liberty and the pursuit of happiness?

    "Unalienable" means that these rights cannot be given away. Because God made us, we are His workmanship and cannot allow ourselves to be destroyed. Because He made us reasonable, we cannot give away the right to be free and to make choices about how to live well. (page 59)
3. What is a "political revolution?"

    One in which a new form of government is instituted, rather than just changing the people who govern. (page 60)
4. "[Locke] is strong on rights, but weak on ends." (page 61) Compare this statement about Locke with the Declaration.

    Locke emphasized that government is for protecting individual rights. The Declaration moves beyond this by speaking of the "ends" of government, and by naming "happiness" as one of the ends. (page 61)
5. Why does the Declaration consider the dictates of prudence before declaring independence?

    The Declaration needed to show that people were not acting as a mob but, being capable of self-government, they were also capable of deliberately acting for their welfare. So it needed to show that revolution was not just a right, but a duty. (page 62) *Also, revolutions can make things worse or even lead to a bloodbath; they are dangerous.* (page 63)
6. Why does the Declaration state that the "legislative powers [are] incapable of annihilation"?

    Men are entitled to government by God and nature; law-making is so fundamental to humanity that authority to make laws cannot be destroyed. (page 64)

Chapter 5 Review Questions

1. Identify at least two aspects of the Articles of Confederation that indicate that the Union was more than an alliance.

   The States are bound to obey Congressional legislation in perpetuity. Granting the "privileges and immunities" of citizens in one state to those of any other aims to build friendship and unity. The acts that the Declaration identifies as proper to "Free and Independent States" are all given to the federal Congress and denied to the States.
2. Why do the Articles insist that the States remain independent?

   The people believed that the State governments were adequate for most of the necessary tasks of government; the federal government is to be strictly limited in what it can do, leaving the states independent in all other areas. (page 77)
3. According to the Articles, which body has "full Power to levy War, conclude Peace, contract Alliances, establish Commerce"?

   The Congress of the United States. (page 78)
4. What does Washington imply was the chief mistake Congress made in the governmental structure set up under the Articles, and why did Americans make that mistake?

   Washington implies that the powers appropriate to the federal government were not "fully and effectually" given to it by the Articles, because the states feared to give such power to a single body of men. (page 81)
5. What does Washington identify as "the greatest interest of every true American" and the immediate goal of the Constitution?

   Washington names "the consolidation of our Union" as the goal. (page 82)
6. Who established the Constitution? How does this compare to the agents of the Articles?

   The People of the several states established the Constitution; the state legislatures established the Articles. (page 83)
7. How does the Constitution "establish Justice"?

   The Constitution institutes the rule of law among its people. A public, established law, not force, settles disputes. (page 84)
8. The Declaration of Independence states that people form governments to "effect their safety and happiness." Which parts of the Preamble to the Constitution show it is established for the safety of the people? For their happiness?

   Safety: "Ensure domestic tranquility; Provide for the common defense." Happiness: "Promote the general welfare; Secure the blessings of liberty."

9. What, in general, are the "Blessings of Liberty"?

Whatever proceeds from the free choice and cooperation of private men can be considered a blessing of liberty. (page 86)

10. What branches of the federal government are most directly connected to the people? Why?

The House of Representatives is directly elected by the people, because it is the source of legislation regarding taxation. The Electors who choose the President can be elected directly by the people, because he wields the power to enforce, to punish. (page 89)

11. *Federalist 59* says: "the abuse of liberty is a greater danger than the abuse of power." How would this explain the following aspects of the Constitution?

    a) Representative government rather than direct democracy

    Representative government allows for deliberation by a small body of men who have time to find out all the facts before reaching a decision.

    b) Election of Senators by State legislatures

    Indirect election of the Senate prevents major changes from being made by the people as soon as the supporters of that change win one election of the House.

    c) Separation of the powers of government by legislative, executive, and judicial branches

    The separation of powers ensures that effective legislation can only occur through the agreement of all three branches, providing more insurance that actions taken are deliberate. (page 89)

    Each of these demands that the people continue to want something for a long time in order to enact important changes in legislation. Time allows for deliberation. Popular governments have always been prone to hasty, passionate decisions that lead to great errors.

12. How does the Constitution attempt to ensure that government works for the good of the whole people?

Equal representation in the Senate, and the election of the President by Electors chosen according to state rather than by a simple majority of the people in the nation help ensure that no one region can dominate the federal government. (page 92)

13. According to Richard Henry Lee, what is the purpose of the Bill of Rights?

The Bill of Rights alerts the people to transgressions of liberty by the government so that they can act to correct them. (page 96)

14. Why might the Bill of Rights be dangerous to liberty? How did the first Congress act to overcome this danger?

    The Bill of Rights might be taken to imply that government has powers that it does not. The first Congress passed the Ninth and Tenth Amendments to make it clear that the other amendments do not imply powers not expressly given. (page 97)
15. How does the Declaration of Independence help us avoid erroneous interpretations of the First Amendment?

    Since the Declaration states that our fundamental rights come from God, interpretations that would prevent public recognition of God or treat religion as a public enemy must be false. (page 100)
16. What is the purpose of the Second Amendment?

    The Second Amendment sustains the practical possibility of rebellion against a tyrannical government. (page 101)

Chapter 6 Review Questions

1. What were the original Constitutional provisions with respect to slavery?

   The Constitution originally counted slaves as 3/5th persons for the purposes of representation and taxation, guaranteed that slaves who escaped to free states would be returned to slavery, and prevented Congress from banning the importation of new slaves until 1808.
2. How did Jefferson refer to the slaves in the first draft of the Declaration? How does the Constitution refer to them?

   Jefferson referred to them as having "human nature," as "persons," and as "men." (page 108) *The Constitution referred to them as "persons," never as "slaves."*
3. What did Levi Hart refer to as a "self-contradiction"?

   That Americans fighting for liberty should hold other men as slaves he called a self-contradiction. (page 109)
4. What did Jefferson tell James Heaton that the ending of slavery required?

   It required a "revolution in public opinion." (page 112)
5. What percentage of the population of South Carolina were slaves at the time of the Constitution?

   More than 50% of the population were slaves in 1789. (page 114)
6. What did South Carolina and the other slave states gain in the Constitution? What did they fail to get? What did the anti-slavery men gain?

   The slave states gained a) a fugitive slave clause, b) slave importation allowed until 1808, c) slaves counting as three-fifths persons for representation and taxes. They failed to get the word "legally" used to describe slavery; they accepted "person" as describing slaves. The anti-slavery men ensured that Congress was not prohibited from eventually banning slavery. (page 116)

7. What factors led anti-slavery men to expect eventual end of slavery?

   a) They expected the white population in the South to increase more quickly than the blacks, making emancipation thinkable; b) the lands available for profitable, slave-based agriculture were limited; c) slavery had already been banned in the Northwest Territories; d) slavery lacked respectability even in the South. (page 117)

8. What did Alexander Stephens call "the cornerstone" of the Confederacy?

   "The great truth that the Negro is not equal to the white man; that slavery... is the normal condition." (page 123)

Chapter 7 Review Questions

1. What did Abraham Lincoln say about the role of the Declaration in his life?

   "I have never had a feeling politically that did not spring from the sentiment embodied in the Declaration of Independence."

2. Answer the following with quotations from Lincoln's speech to the Young Men's Lyceum:

   a) "The alienation of their affections from the government is the natural consequence" of what?

      If the laws be continually despised and disregarded, if their rights to be secure in their persons and property, are held by no better tenure than the caprice of the mob... " (page 131)

   b) "While ever a state of feeling, such as this, shall... very generally prevail throughout the nation, vain will be every effort... to subvert our national freedom." To what "state of feeling" does Lincoln refer?

      He refers to "reverence for the laws." (page 132)

   c) "It thirsts and burns for distinction, and, if possible, it will have it, whether at the expense of emancipating slaves, or enslaving freemen." What is it?

      The "towering genius" of ambitious men. (page 133)

   d) "It will in future be an enemy." What is it?

      Passion. (page 135)

3. This chapter and the last refer to historical events crucial for understanding the Declaration Statesmanship of the founders, Abraham Lincoln, Martin Luther King, Jr., and others. To help see the relationship between

these events, construct a timeline incorporating the following events. You may use other references to find dates.

The order of events on the time line will be as follows:

- (a) First Congressional ban on the importation of slaves. 1776
- (d) Jefferson proposes abolition of slavery in Virginia. 1778
- (c) Pennsylvania passes a gradual emancipation law. 1780
- (b) Northwest Ordinance outlaws slavery in Federal territories. 1787
- (f) Slave trade ended by U.S. Congress. 1808
- (j) Missouri Compromise. 1820
- (e) Jefferson and Madison die. July 4, 1826
- (g) Lincoln's speech to the Young Men's Lyceum. 1838
- (m) Compromise which allowed admission of Calif. as a free state. 1850
- (k) *Uncle Tom's Cabin.* 1851
- (o) Repeal of the Missouri Compromise. 1854
- (i) Lincoln's Peoria Speech. 1854
- (h) *Dred Scott* decision. 1858
- (q) Lincoln-Douglas debates. 1858
- (n) Lincoln's First Inaugural. 1861
- (l) Gettysburg Address. 1863
- (r) Lincoln's Second Inaugural. 1865
- (p) Lincoln assassinated. 1865
- (s) Black Codes enacted. 1865
- (v) Fourteenth Amendment passed. 1868
- (y) Jim Crow Laws enacted. 1890-1910
- (w) *Plessy v. Ferguson.* 1896
- (z) Segregation of federal workplaces in Washington, D.C. 1913
- (u) *Brown v. Board of Education.* 1954
- (x) Martin Luther King, Jr.'s, 'I Have a Dream' speech. 1963
- (t) *Regents of Univ. of Ca. v. Bakke.* 1978

4. What did Lincoln see as the three chief goods of the Missouri Compromise?

   Lincoln saw its chief goods as, a) the fact of territory free of slavery north of the 36°30′ *line, b) the right of Congress to forbid slavery in the territories, c) the moral disapprobation of slavery through outlawing it in the territories.* (page 145)

5. Of what did Emerson write: "I will not obey it, by God!"

   The fugitive slave law. (page 147)

6. What is the "great principle" of the American republic proclaimed by Stephen Douglas? How did he think this principle would help save the Union? How did it differ from the principle of the founders?

    His great principle was "Popular Sovereignty," that is, "the right of every community to judge and decide of itself whether a thing is right or wrong." (page 149) *He thought it would save the Union by making a divisive national discussion of slavery unnecessary.* (page 151) *Douglas made self-rule, not self-evident truths, the deepest principle of a free government.* (page 153)
7. What did Lincoln say is the leading principle of American Republicanism?

    "No man is good enough to govern another man without that other's consent." (page 154)
8. What does Thomas West say "will more often lead to misery and terror than [to] justice and happiness"?

    "The immoderate pursuit of moral perfection." (page 158)
9. What did Lincoln think prevented the social and political equality of the white and black races?

    Public opinion driven by sentiment, feeling, and passion, prevented full equality. (page 159)
10. What were the key elements of the *Dred Scott* decision? How did the decision threaten Douglas's great principle? How did Lincoln react to the decision?

    The key elements in the Dred Scott decision were that Congress never had a right to prohibit slavery in the territories, and that blacks could not be citizens of the United States. (page 164) *The decision overturned Douglas's "Popular Sovereignty" because it denied that territories could ban slavery.* (page 166) *Lincoln accepted the decision but pledged to overturn it; he quoted Andrew Jackson's claim that each branch of government has to follow the Constitution as it understands it.* (page 168)

Chapter 8 Review Questions

1. What were the "black codes"?

    The black codes were laws passed by the reconstructed Southern governments that restricted blacks' freedom of contract, travel, and employment. (page 179)
2. What did the Fourteenth Amendment promise the freed blacks? Why was its authority questioned in the South?

    The Fourteenth Amendment guaranteed to blacks and other minorities the rights of citizenship and equal treatment under the law. (page 180)

The Southern states questioned its authority because they were forced to approve it as a condition of readmittance to the Union. (page 180)

3. What percentage of colored voters were there in Louisiana in 1904 compared to 1896? What caused the drop?

   1,342 to 130,334 = 1%. The increased violence and power of the white workingmen and small farmers intimidated blacks; the populist movements later passed laws greatly restricting black access to voting. (page 185)
4. What philosophies contributed to a 'respectable' racism in the Progressive Movement?

   Social Darwinism, German Historicism, and social sciences (biology, sociology, and anthropology).
5. What notable success did McKinley achieve in Congress? What did he give up for it?

   He was able to push through a new tariff bill (and the Sherman Silver Purchase Act.) He gave up a much needed voting rights bill.
6. Why did Justice Harlan dissent from the majority opinion in *Plessy v. Ferguson?*

   He believed the majority opinion recognized "a power in the states to interfere with the full enjoyment of the blessings of liberty. . . " (page 199)
7. Why did the Court in *Brown v. Board of Education* overturn racial segregation in schools? Why did the NAACP argue that it should be overturned?

   The Court argued that psychological harm might be inflicted on children under segregation; the NAACP argued that the Fourteenth Amendment declares the Constitution to be color-blind. (page 200)
8. Why did Booker T. Washington encourage submissive patience in the face of discrimination?

   Washington thought that the friendship of white neighbors was a surer protection than the Federal government, and he thought it was what Christ taught and practiced. (page 204)
9. What did the Niagara Movement declare to be the "way to liberty"?

   "Persistent manly agitation is the way to liberty." (page 205)
10. What was the name of Martin Luther King's own organization? What was its motto?

    His organization was the Southern Christian Leadership Conference, and its motto was "To save the soul of America."

Chapter 9 Review Questions

There are no review questions for chapter 9.

Questions from the Book of Readings

Questions are on their own pages, so that they may be copied and given to students who are not using our *Book of Readings.*

Articles of Confederation — Questions

1. Give the number of the article that deals with each of the following:
   a) What States may not do.
   b) Procedures for electing members of Congress.
   c) How taxes shall be determined and calculated.
   d) What Congress may do.
   e) How individual States shall relate to the free inhabitants of other States.
   f) That the Congress shall have limited powers.
   g) The Assumption of debts incurred by the Continental Congress.
   h) How the Articles can be amended.
   i) The purpose of the Confederation.
2. How many branches does the federal government established by the Articles have?
3. Find quotations to answer the following questions.
   a) How does Congress make decisions about declaring war, or borrowing money?
   b) How many representatives does each State have? How many votes?
   c) How many States need to agree to make an alteration in the Articles?
   d) How long shall the Articles be in effect?
4. "Each State retains its sovereignty, freedom, and independence, and every power, jurisdiction, and right, which is not by this Confederation expressly delegated to the United States in Congress assembled." (Article II) Which of the following powers are "expressly delegated" to the Congress?
   a) declaring war
   b) making treaties
   c) regulating coin
   d) collecting taxes
   e) raising and equipping the army
   f) building and equipping a navy

Articles of Confederation — Answers

1. a) *Art. VI*
   b) *Art. V*
   c) *Art. VIII*
   d) *Art. IX*
   e) *Art. IV*
   f) *Art. II*
   g) *Art. XII*
   h) *Art. XIII*
   i) *Art. III*
2. *One, the Congress.*
3. a) *"The United States in Congress assembled shall never engage in war... nor borrow money on the credit of the United States... unless nine States assent to the same... " Article IX*
   b) *"No State shall be represented in Congress by less than two, nor more than seven members... In determining questions in the United States in Congress assembled, each State shall have one vote." Article V*
   c) *"... nor shall any alteration at any time hereafter be made in any of them; unless such alteration be agreed to in a Congress of the United States, and be afterwards confirmed by the legislatures of every State." Article XIII*
   d) *"And the Articles of this Confederation shall be inviolably observed by every State, and the Union shall be perpetual... " Article XIII*
4. *a (making war), b (making treaties), c (regulating coin), and f (building and equipping a navy); (See Article IX. But note how difficult it is to be certain.)*

The Constitution — Questions

1. How many purposes of the Constitution are enumerated in the Preamble?
2. Give a title to each of the sections of Article I.
3. Article I, section 8, begins by giving Congress the power to raise funds for two of the purposes mentioned in the Preamble: "provide for the common defence and general welfare of the United States". Which of the powers enumerated in the remainder of section 8 pertain to the common defense? Which pertain to the general welfare? Is Congress granted powers relating to the other four purposes mentioned in the Preamble?
4. What does section 7 say is peculiar to the House of the Representatives?
5. According to section 7, who has to agree to a bill before it becomes a law? Do all of them always have to agree before a bill becomes a law?
6. Define each of the following terms as used in the Constitution:
   a) Writ of habeas corpus
   b) Bill of attainder
   c) Ex post facto law
   d) Impeachment
   e) Duty
7. Consider sections 2 and 3. Contrast the House with the Senate with respect to
   a) qualifications for office
   b) terms
   c) number for each state
   d) impeachment
   e) leader
8. Write a title for each of the articles of the Constitution.
9. Who elects the President? What is his term for office? What qualifications must a man have to be eligible to become President?
10. Name three chief powers of the President.
11. Who appoints judges? What is their term of office?

The Constitution — Answers

1. *Six: to form a more perfect union, establish justice, ensure domestic tranquillity, provide for the common defense, promote the general welfare and secure the blessings of liberty to ourselves and our posterity.*
2. a) *Legislative powers vested in a Congress with two houses*
   b) *Composition of the House and election of its members*
   c) *Composition of the Senate and election of its members*
   d) *Times, places, and manners of Congressional elections and meetings*
   e) *Procedures applying to both houses*
   f) *Regulations regarding individual senators and representatives*
   g) *How laws are made*
   h) *Powers granted to Congress*
   i) *Prohibitions on the powers of Congress*
   j) *Prohibitions on the powers of the States*
3. *The next eight seem to pertain to the general welfare (although the eighth, "To constitute tribunals inferior to the Supreme Court," might rather pertain to establishing justice); the seven following these pertain to the common defense; the last two might be considered part of the establishment of the Constitution itself.*
4. *"All bills for raising revenue shall originate in the House of Representatives."*
5. *The House and Senate must both pass the bill, and then the President must sign it. However, a bill will become a law automatically, if the President decides not to sign it within 10 days of receiving it; or, if he vetoes the bill, it can become law if both the House and Senate repass it with a 2/3 majority in both houses.*
6. a) *a court order that directs an official holding someone in custody to produce the prisoner together with evidence to justify his confinement (Article I, section 9)*
   b) *a law punishing relatives or associates of persons convicted of treason (Article I, sections 9 and 10,)*
   c) *a law making an action criminal after it has been done (Article I, sections 9 and 10)*
   d) *a special indictment of an official for misdeeds committed while in office, which is followed by a trial on those charges (Article I, sections 2 and 3; Article II, sections 2 and 4, Article 3, section 2)*
   e) *a payment levied on the import, export, manufacture, or sale of goods (Article I, section 9 and 10)*

7\.

	HOUSE	SENATE
a.	*25 years old, 7 years a citizen*	*30 years old, 9 years a citizen*
b.	*2 year term*	*6 year term*
c.	*Determined by the number of free persons, plus 3/5 of all others*	*Two Senators for each state*
d.	*The House has sole power of impeachment*	*The Senate has sole power to try all impeachments*
e.	*The House chooses its Speaker*	*The Vice President is the president of the Senate*

8\.
- Article I *On the legislative power.*
- Article II *On the executive power.*
- Article III *On the judicial power.*
- Article IV *Relationships between the States and other entities.*
- Article V *How to amend the Constitution.*
- Article VI *The authority of the Constitution.*
- Article VII *Establishing the Constitution.*

9\. *The President is elected by electors appointed by each State; the number of electors for each State is equal to the number of its Representatives plus its Senators. He is elected for a term of four years. He must be a natural-born citizen of the United States, 35 years old, and 14 years a resident of the United States.*

10\.
- *The President is commander-in-chief of the army and navy*
- *He has the power to make treaties (by and with the advice and consent of the Senate)*
- *He appoints ambassadors, judges of the Supreme Court, and all other officers of the United States (by and with the advice and consent of the Senate)*

11\. *Judges are appointed by the President with the Senate; they are appointed "during good behavior," that is, for life, unless they behave in such a way as to be impeached.*

The Amendments — Questions

1. How are amendments to the Constitution proposed and ratified?
2. The first amendment to the Constitution prohibits Congress from doing six things. What are they?
3. According to the second amendment, why shall "the right to keep and bear arms" not be infringed?
4. How does the fourth amendment try to prevent "unreasonable searches and seizures"?
5. Which amendments protect the rights of suspected criminals?
6. Are the ninth and tenth amendments about different things?
7. Identify the article and section number in the body of the Constitution that were altered by the following:
   a) Twelfth Amendment
   b) Sixteenth Amendment
   c) Seventeenth Amendment
8. Which amendment first defined "citizen of the United States"? Which first allowed women to vote? Which allowed citizens 18 years old to vote?

The Amendments — Answers

1. *Amendments are proposed either by Congress, "whenever two thirds of both houses shall deem it necessary," or by a convention called for by the legislatures of two-thirds of the States; to become part of the Constitution, they must be ratified by three-fourths of the States.*
2. *Congress shall make no law*
   1) *respecting the establishment of religion,*
   2) *prohibiting the free exercise of religion,*
   3) *abridging the freedom of speech,*
   4) *abridging the freedom of the press,*
   5) *abridging the right of the people to peaceably assemble,*
   6) *abridging the right of the people to petition the government for a redress of grievances.*
3. *Because a well regulated militia is necessary to the security of free State.*
4. *It demands that search warrants be issued only for probable cause, with supporting oaths, and details of what exactly is going to be done.*
5. *Amendments four, five, six, and eight.*
6. *Yes. The ninth amendment is about the rights of the people; the tenth is about the powers of the States and the people.*
7. a) *Art. II, sect. 1*
   b) *Art. I, sect. 2*
   c) *Art. I, sect. 3*
8. *Amend. XIV, Amend. XIX, Amend. XXVI*

Federalist No. 1 — Questions

1. Lincoln spoke of the Civil War as a test. Publius speaks of "the important question" that Americans have to decide. What is the question?
2. "History will teach us that the former has been found a much more certain road to the introduction of despotism than the latter. . . " What are the "former" and the "latter?"
3. "In the course of the preceding observations, I have had an eye, my fellow-citizens, to putting you upon your guard against all attempts, from whatever quarter, to influence your decision. . . by any impressions other than those which may result from the evidence of truth." What other "impressions" does Publius fear might influence their decision?

Question for General Discussion:

Publius says, "You will, no doubt, at the same time, have collected from the general scope of [my observations] that they proceed from a source not unfriendly to the new Constitution." What observations in particular show that Publius favors the adoption of the Constitution? What do these say about the differing sides in the debate over adoption?

Federalist No. 1 — Answers

1. *"...whether societies of men are really capable or not of establishing good government from reflection and choice, or whether they are forever destined to depend for their political constitutions on accident and force."*
2. *The former is "zeal for the rights of the people;" the latter is "zeal for the firmness and efficiency of government."*
3. *Publius fears passions, prejudice, anger, ambition, avarice, personal animosity, party opposition, and jealousy for the rights of the people, among other things.*

Federalist No. 2 — Questions

1. What, according to Publius, "has until lately been a received and uncontradicted opinion?"
2. Publius says: "I have as often taken notice that Providence has been pleased to give this one connected country to one united people." Name three of the six reasons he gives for speaking of the people as one and united.
3. According to Publius, what "must ever precede the formation of a wise and well-balanced government for a free people?"
4. What will cause America to exclaim: "FAREWELL! A LONG FAREWELL TO ALL MY GREATNESS"?

Question for General Discussion:

According to Publius, does government make a people one, or does one people form a government?

Federalist No. 2 — Answers

1. *"It has until lately been a received and uncontradicted opinion that the prosperity of the people of America depended on their continuing firmly united. . . "*
2. *They are a people: 1) "descended from the same ancestors," 2) "speaking the same language," 3) "professing the same religion," 4) "attached to the same principles of government," 5) "very similar in their manners and customs," and 6) "who, by their joint counsels, arms, and efforts, fighting side by side throughout a long and bloody war, have nobly established general liberty and independence."*
3. *". . . Calm and mature inquiries and reflections."*
4. *". . . Whenever the dissolution of the Union arrives. . . "*

Federalist No. 9 — Questions

1. "The advocates of despotism... have decried all free government as inconsistent with the order of society..." Why?
2. Publius claims that improvements in the science of politics has made republican government more perfect. What five improvements does he name?

Federalist No. 9 — Answers

1. *The disorders among the "petty republics of Greece and Italy" with their "perpetual vibration between the extremes of tyranny and anarchy" led the enemies of free government to condemn them.*
2. - *"The regular distribution of power into distinct departments;"*
   - *"the introduction of legislative balances and checks;"*
   - *"the institution of courts composed of judges holding their offices during good behavior;"*
   - *"the representation of the people in the legislature by deputies of their own election;"*
   - *"the ENLARGEMENT of the ORBIT within which such systems are to revolve..."*

Federalist Nos. 15 & 16 — Questions

1. What principle is said to be "…evidently incompatible with idea of *government*"?
2. What "scheme would indeed be pernicious… but would have the merit of being, at least, consistent and practicable?" To what is this scheme being contrasted?
3. Complete the following: Government implies ______________, which implies __________.
4. Complete the following: "In an association where the general authority is confined to the collective bodies of the communities that compose it, __________."
5. How does Publius answer this rhetorical question: "Why has government been instituted at all?"

Federalist Nos. 15 & 16 — Answers

1. *The principle is that of "Legislation for States or Governments, in their corporate or collective capacities, and as contradistinguished from the individuals of which they consist."*
2. *"There is nothing absurd or impracticable in the idea of a league or alliance between independent nations... " This is contrasted to "a national government, or, which is the same thing... a superintending power, under the direction of a common council... "*
3. Government implies *the power of making laws*, which implies *a penalty or punishment for disobedience.*
4. "In an association where the general authority is confined to the collective bodies of the communities that compose it, *every breach of the laws must involve a state of war...*"
5. *Because the passions of men will not conform to the dictates of reason and justice, without constraint."*

Federalist No. 84 — Questions

1. What "have been, in all ages, the favorite and most formidable instruments of tyranny"? What restrictions in the body of the Constitution are directed against these instruments?
2. Publius claims that a "minute detail of particular rights is certainly far less applicable to a Constitution like that under consideration... " than to the constitution of New York. Why?
3. Publius thinks that the freedom of the press really relies on what?

Question for General Discussion:

Is Publius right to affirm that "bills of rights... are not only unnecessary in the proposed Constitution, but would even be dangerous"?

Federalist No. 84 — Answers

1. *"... the subjecting of men to punishment for things which, when they were done, were breaches of no law, and the practice of arbitrary imprisonments, have been in all ages, the favorite and most formidable instruments of tyranny." The body of the Constitution forbids Congress from making ex post facto laws against the first and establishes a writ of habeas corpus against the second.*
2. *The Constitution of the United States is "merely intended to regulate the general political interests of the nation... " while New York's constitution "has the regulation of every species of personal and private concerns."*
3. *The liberty of the press "must altogether depend on public opinion, and on the general spirit of the people and of the government."*

Democracy in America: first reading — Questions

1. Tocqueville says that religion "regulates the state." How does it do this?
2. "There is certainly no country in the world where the tie of marriage is more respected than in America..." Why is this important for maintaining democracy?
3. Religion in America prevents Americans from advancing what "impious adage which seems to have been invented in an age of freedom to shelter all future tyrants"?
4. What is Tocqueville implying when he rhetorically asks, "How is it possible that society should escape destruction if the moral tie is not strengthened in proportion as the political tie is relaxed?"
5. Why did the Constitution of New York forbid clergy from holding public office (see footnote 3)?
6. Speaking of freedom of religion, Tocqueville was led "to inquire how it happened that real authority of religion was increased by a state of things which diminished its apparent force." Briefly, what is his answer?
7. What is the novel condition of society that tempted Tocqueville "to burn my book to apply none but novel ideas..."?
8. How do Americans primarily learn about laws and forms of government?

For Discussion: "Religion in America... must be regarded as the first of their political institutions; for if it does not impart a taste for freedom, it facilitates the use of it." How does religion "facilitate the use" of freedom? If this is true, should religion be considered a matter of public concern in America?

Democracy in America: first reading — Answers

1. *"In the United States religion exercises but little influence upon the laws and upon the details of pubic opinion; but it directs the customs of the community. . . "*
2. *The happiness Americans find at home teaches them "that an orderly life is the surest path to happiness. . . which he afterwards carries with him into public affairs."*
3. *"Hitherto no one in the United States has dared to advance the maxim that everything is permissible for the interests of society. . . "*
4. *He implies that the more free men are from the restrictions of law, the more they must be committed within to living a moral life, "if society is to avoid destruction."*
5. *". . . The ministers of the Gospel. . . ought not to be diverted from the great duties of their functions. . . "*
6. *The real source of religious devotion is found in man's natural desire for a future life. When religion allies itself with a political power, it makes its own authority become as transient as that of the political power.*
7. *Americans are almost universally educated but have few men who are really learned.*
8. *"The American learns to know the laws by participating in the act of legislation; and he takes a lesson in the forms of government from governing."*

Democracy in America: second reading — Questions

1. "Despotism, then, which is at all times dangerous, is more particularly to be feared in democratic ages." Why?
2. In what way do Americans combat democratic individualism?
3. Why does de Tocqueville think Americans attend to the public interest?
4. Why do Americans form private associations for every sort of undertaking?
5. What do Tocqueville's countrymen think should be done to correct for individual weakness in democratic societies? Why does he disagree with them?
6. "The progress of all the rest depends on the progress it has made." What is it on which the progress of all the rest depends?

Democracy in America: second reading — Answers

1. *Equality keeps men separated from one another, involved in their own interest. Despotism "sees in the separation among men the surest guarantee of its continuance, and it usually makes every effort to keep them separate."*
2. *Americans have combated this by free institutions, particularly by leaving most affairs in the hands of local districts. This encourages men to get involved in local politics, leading them "to value the affection of their neighbors and of their kindred..."*
3. *Both because it is in their own interest, and because they develop a sense of duty and a taste for serving their fellow citizens.*
4. *While aristocratic noblemen can compel their subordinates, men in democratic societies are independent and feeble.*
5. *His countrymen think the government should do what individual men can't do. Tocqueville thinks government can never do it all, and that the more it does, the less individuals are inclined to form associations for performing other activities.*
6. *The science of association.*

Peoria Speech: Part I — Questions

1. "Thus, with the author of the Declaration of Independence, the policy of prohibiting slavery in the new territory originated." What does Lincoln mean by this?
2. What was the Missouri Compromise?
3. What was the Wilmot Proviso? Was it ever made law?
4. Name six "adjustments" that the Compromise of 1850 made with respect to slavery.
5. What did Judge Douglas replace the Missouri Compromise with?

Peoria Speech: Part I — Answers

1. *Jefferson prevailed on Virginia to cede its territory in the Northwest to Congress provided that slavery be prohibited there.*
2. *The Missouri Compromise allowed Missouri to enter the Union as a slave state, but outlawed slavery in all the rest of the Louisiana Purchase north of the* 36°30′ *line.*
3. *The Wilmot Proviso was an amendment that would have banned slavery in any territory acquired from Mexico. It was never passed; eventually the territory was acquired without the Senate ever approving the amendment.*
4. *The South got a more efficient fugitive slave law, an allowance for Utah and New Mexico to decide whether to become free or slave states (though the federal government could still ban slavery while they remained territories), and $10,000,000 for Texas to pay off her debts; the North got California admitted as a free state, the slave trade abolished in the District of Columbia, and Texas's boundary moved eastward.*
5. *Douglas repealed the Missouri Compromise for Kansas and Nebraska, instead allowing the territories to decide for themselves whether they would have slavery or not.*

Peoria Speech: Part II — Questions

1. Why does Lincoln hate indifference to slavery?
2. Lincoln says of the states where slavery already exists, "... that it is very difficult to get rid of [slavery], in any satisfactory way, I can understand and appreciate... " Here are three possibilities he considers. What difficulty does he see with each of them?
   a) "My first impulse would be to free all and send them to Liberia—to their own native land."
   b) "What then? Free them all, and keep them among us as underlings?"
   c) "What next? Free them, and make them politically and socially, our equals?"
3. Douglas justified the repeal of the Missouri Compromise by saying that it had already been repealed in principle by 1) the Wilmot Proviso and 2) the provision of 1850 allowing Utah and New Mexico to be admitted as free or slave states according to their choice. How does Lincoln answer this claim?
4. Why does Lincoln think it crucial to keep slavery out of the Kansas and Nebraska territories?
5. Lincoln says, "In all these cases, it is your sense of justice, and human sympathy, continually telling you, that the poor negro has some natural right to himself... " To what cases does he refer?

Peoria Speech: Part II — Answers

1. *1) Slavery is a monstrous injustice; 2) slavery "deprives our republican example of its just influence in the world," causing the enemies of liberty to call us hypocrites, the friends of liberty to doubt our sincerity; 3) slavery forces good men into an open war with fundamental principles of civil liberty as found in the Declaration of Independence.* (page 189)
2. a) *This could not be done suddenly, because of the difficulties of ships, supplies and money.*
   b) *It is not certain they would be better off.*
   c) *The feelings of the great mass of white people would not admit of this.*
3. 1) *The* 36°30′ *line was only meant to apply to the old Louisiana territory; the Wilmot Proviso attempted to exclude slavery from all new territory, without touching the particular compromise regarding the Louisiana territory.*
   2) *The anti-slavery men compromised about Utah and New Mexico because they got something else they wanted in exchange. If the Missouri Compromise is to be repealed, the North should get something in return.*
4. *Lincoln believed that if slavery was forbidden until a territory was ready to become a state, no territory would actually vote to bring it in. But if slavery was not forbidden, slave owners would bring their slaves into the territory, making it very difficult to outlaw it.*
5. 1) *The South joined with the North to ban the African slave trade and to punish violators of it by death;*
   2) *Southerners despised slave dealers;*
   3) *Southerners recognized the freedom of over 400,000 blacks, even though they could have made a lot of money by enslaving them.*

Peoria Speech: Part III — Questions

1. Lincoln says, "The doctrine of self-government is right — absolutely and eternally right..." Why does he deny the territories the right to govern themselves in the matter of slavery?
2. What four reasons does Lincoln give showing that the extension of slavery into the territories is a question for the whole people, and not just for the settlers?
3. Why does the repeal of the Missouri Compromise threaten the Union?
4. "The spirit of seventy-six and the spirit of Nebraska are utter antagonisms." What are these "spirits"?

Questions for General Discussion:

1. "The repeal of the Missouri Compromise, and the propriety of its restoration, constitute the subject of what I am about to say." If Lincoln thinks it was right to compromise on so important a question as slavery, how can he still pretend really to believe that slavery is a "monstrous injustice"? Look at both the Missouri Compromise and the Compromise of 1850.
2. Lincoln argues that the repeal of the Missouri Compromise on the basis of "the sacred right of self-government" would lead to an insistence "that there is no right principle of action but self-interest." Does Lincoln make an effective argument that these two are connected?

Peoria Speech: Part III — Answers

1. *Lincoln argued that if the negro is a man, then slavery is a total destruction of self-government because it denies the right of a man to govern himself.*
2. a) *The territories should be available for poor whites from all the states to settle, not for slave owners and their slaves.*
   b) *Northerners have a Constitutional obligation to return fugitive slaves to their owners.*
   c) *Slaves give states that have them a proportionately greater representation that free states have.*
   d) *The extension of slavery is a great danger to the liberties and institutions of the whole people.*
3. *The slavery question had been settled for all existing territories by the two Compromises. The repeal of the Missouri Compromise raises the dangerous question again by making the extension of slavery possible. The natural love of justice will fight to keep slavery from spreading.*
4. *The spirit of seventy-six is the belief that "all men are created equal;" the spirit of Nebraska is the view that the right to own slaves is a sacred right of self-government.*

Speech on *Dred Scott* — Questions

1. The *Dred Scott* decision declares what two propositions?
2. What does Lincoln think that the role of the decisions of the Supreme Court on Constitutional matters should be?
3. Which of the following does Lincoln imply raise doubts about the precedent value of *Dred Scott*?
   a) It was not a unanimous decision.
   b) It was not made in Washington, D.C.
   c) Partisan bias was involved.
   d) It was based on errors about historical facts.
   e) The President and Congress did not agree with the Supreme Court.
4. Lincoln quotes Judge Curtis, one of the Supreme Court Justices who dissented from the *Dred Scott* decision, who argues that negroes were a part of the people for whom the Declaration of Independence and the Constitution were made. What evidence does he give?
5. Taney and Douglas disagree with Lincoln about what the Declaration meant when it said "all men are created equal." How did each of these man understand the phrase?

Question for General Discussion:

Lincoln says, "We believe, as much as Judge Douglas, (perhaps more) in obedience to, and respect for the Judicial department of government." Is this statement consistent with his view of the *Dred Scott* decision?

Speech on *Dred Scott* — Answers

1. *The* Dred Scott *decision declares that a negro cannot sue in the United States courts and that Congress cannot prohibit slavery in the Territories.*
2. *to absolutely determine the particular case before them, and to establish precedents indicating how similar cases will be judged. He does not think that they should always or finally determine policy.*
3. *a, c, d.*
4. *Judge Curtis points out that five of the original thirteen states allowed free blacks to vote at the time of the Constitution.*
5. *Taney denied that it applied to negroes because the founders did not immediately free the slaves. Douglas held that "men" only referred to British citizens. Lincoln believed that "men" included negroes, as well as the French, Germans, etc. He thought that Jefferson made the universal claim so that Americans in all generations could aim to make that equality a reality.*

House Divided Speech — Questions

1. Why is this speech referred to as the "House Divided" speech?
2. Lincoln claims that Douglas' doctrine of "the sacred right of self-government" was being used to mold public opinion in the North. What does he mean?
3. "Welcome or unwelcome, such decision is probably coming, and will soon be upon us, unless the power of the present political dynasty shall be met and overthrown. . . " What decision does Lincoln expect?

Question for General Discussion:

Lincoln says that the advocates of slavery "will push it forward till it shall become alike lawful in all the states, old as well as new, North as well as South." Considering the evidence he brings forward in this speech, does it look like Lincoln is acting as statesman wisely reading "the signs of the times" or as politician seeking to attack his opponent, Douglas, unfairly? Consider the roles Lincoln assigns to the four "workmen": Stephen [Douglas], Franklin [Pierce, U.S. President from 1853 to 1857], Roger [Taney, Chief Justice of the Supreme Court, author of the majority opinion in the *Dred Scott* decision], and James [Buchanan, President at the time of the "House Divided" speech].

House Divided Speech — Answers

1. *Lincoln cites the Biblical text, "A house divided against itself cannot stand," then goes on to argue that the Union cannot remain permanently divided into free states and slave states.*
2. *Because Douglas held that the territories should be allowed to decide on the question of slavery for themselves, he avowed that he didn't care if slavery was allowed or not as long as the vote was fairly conducted.* (page 228) *Lincoln held that Douglas' doctrine, the "Nebraska doctrine," was being used to convince Northerners that they shouldn't care about slavery in the territories, either.* (page 229)
3. *Lincoln expects that the Supreme Court will declare "the Constitution of the United States does not permit a state to exclude slavery from its limits."* (page 230)

Gettysburg Address — Questions

1. Lincoln speaks of the Civil War as a "test". What is the test?
2. Lincoln describes our nation in two ways, one at the beginning, the other at the end. What are these ways?

Questions for General Discussion:

Are the two phrases, "conceived in liberty" and "dedicated to the proposition that all men are created equal," connected? In other words, does liberty depend on the view that all men are created equal? If you think all men are created equal, are you likely to conceive a nation in liberty?

Gettysburg Address — Answers

1. *The Civil War is a test to see if a free nation can long endure.*
2. a) *a nation "conceived in liberty and dedicated to the proposition that all men are created equal"*

   b) *a "nation under God," with a "government of the people, by the people, for the people."*

Cornerstone Speech — Questions

1. Stephens thought that the Confederate Constitution improved upon the "old Constitution" in a number of ways. Put the following in the order in which he brings them up in the speech:
   a) It would stop agitation about the slavery question.
   b) It forbade the use of the common treasury for internal improvements that would benefit only one part of the country.
   c) It extended Presidential term to six years, but only allowed the President to serve one term.
   d) It forbade the use of tariffs to favor one branch of industry over another.
   e) It would allow cabinet officers to participate in legislative debates in the House and Senate.
2. What did Stephens claim was the immediate cause of the Confederate revolution?
3. What did the founding generation think of slavery, according to Stephens?
4. What is the "great physical, philosophical, and moral truth" that is the basis of the new, Confederate government?
5. "Our system commits no such violation of nature's laws." To what is Stephens referring?

Cornerstone Speech — Answers

1. (d) *It forbade the use of tariffs to favor one branch of industry over another.*
   (b) *It forbade the use of the common treasury for internal improvements that would benefit only one part of the country.*
   (e) *It would allow cabinet officers to participate in legislative debates in the House and Senate.*
   (c) *It extended Presidential term to six years, but only allowed the President to serve one term.*
   (a) *It would stop agitation about the slavery question.*
2. *The "peculiar institution" of African slavery as it existed in the South.*
3. *"The prevailing ideas entertained by [Jefferson] and most of the leading statesmen at the time of the formation of the old constitution, were that the enslavement of the African was in violation of the laws of nature; that it was wrong in principle, socially, morally, and politically."*
4. *"The negro is not equal to the white man... slavery—subordination to the superior race—is his natural and normal condition."*
5. *"Many governments have been founded upon the principle of the subordination and serfdom of certain classes of the same race; such were and are in violation of the laws of nature."*

Calvin Coolidge: *The Inspiration of the Declaration* — Questions

1. The Declaration of Independence "rises above the ordinary conception of rebellion." Why does Coolidge think this?
2. What makes the Declaration "the most important civil document in the world"?
3. According to Coolidge, where did Thomas Jefferson secure his "best ideas of democracy"?
4. Coolidge compares the principles of the Declaration of Independence with those at the basis of earlier revolutions, such as the Dutch revolt. What does he point out as peculiar to the Declaration? Where does he think this idea came from?
5. Coolidge says, "A spring will cease to flow if its source be dried up; a tree will wither if its roots be destroyed." How does he apply this to America?

For Discussion: What does Coolidge mean by the following: "No other theory is adequate to explain or comprehend the Declaration of Independence. It is the product of the spiritual insight of the people"? Does he give adequate support for this claim?

Calvin Coolidge: *The Inspiration of the Declaration* — Answers

1. *Coolidge emphasizes that the delegates that signed the Declaration were acting in obedience to their own states, their own constituents. This process showed the Declaration was the result of the deliberate thought of the dominant portion of the people, not the act of a small conspiracy nor of a rioting mob.*
2. *The Declaration not only declared the immortal truths that men are created equal, endowed with unalienable rights, and that just government depends on the consent of the governed, but it also effectively brought into being a nation founded on those principles.*
3. *He secured them at church meetings.*
4. *The doctrine of the equality of men "had not before appeared as an official political declaration of any nation." Coolidge thinks it came from the preaching and teaching of the 17th century American clergy, who "preached equality because they believed in the fatherhood of God and the brotherhood of man."*
5. *The ideals of the Declaration are spiritual, not material. "They have their source and roots in the religious convictions. They belong to the unseen world. Unless the faith of the American people in these religious convictions is to endure, the principles of our Declaration will perish."*

Quizzes, Tests, and Answers

The quizzes are printed—one to a page—following this page so they can be photocopied for use.

The tests following the quizzes may be photocopied from this book. If you have multiple students, copy the Student Answer Sheets that follow the tests, and you should find them easier to grade. The Answer Keys for the tests start on page 112.

Quiz 1 Answers [end of chapter 3]

1. b
2. a
3. d
4. e
5. They both refer to attempts of the British Parliament to legislate for the colonies.
6. a, b, e
7. Political power

Quiz 2 Answers [after studying the Constitution in chapter 5]

1. a) two years
   b) six years
   c) four years
   d) "during good behavior," i.e., for life
2. Impeachment; Initiating bills for raising revenue
3. 3/4ths of them
4. a) people
   b) legislators
   c) electors
   d) President (with consent of Senate)

Quiz 3 Answers [end of chapter 7]

1. The "3/5ths clause" regarding representation and taxation;
2. the "fugitive slave clause;"
3. and the clause preventing Congress from banning slavery before 1808.
4. The Missouri Compromise
5. Popular Sovereignty
6. 1787 (The Northwest Ordinance)

Quiz 1 10 points total

Put the following statements in the order in which they appear in the *Declaration of Independence*, and then answer the questions that follow (1 point each).

a. "We, therefore, the Representatives of the United States of America... do, in the Name, and by the authority of the good People of these Colonies, solemnly publish and declare: That these United Colonies are, and of Right ought to be Free and Independent States..."

b. "...A decent respect to the opinions of mankind requires that they should declare the causes which impel them to the separation."

c. "He has refused his Assent to Laws, the most wholesome and necessary for the public good."

d. "We hold these truths to be self-evident, that all men are created equal, that they are endowed by their Creator with certain unalienable Rights..."

e. "The history of the present King of Great Britain is a history of repeated injuries and usurpations, all having in direct object the establishment of an absolute Tyranny over these States. To prove this, let Facts be submitted to a candid world."

1. Which comes first of all?
2. Which comes last?
3. Which is first, c or d?
4. Which is first, c or e?
5. The following quotations from the Declaration express one of the major complaints of the American colonists. Restate it in more familiar language. (2 points)

   "He has combined with others to subject us to a jurisdiction foreign to our constitution and unacknowledged by our laws..." "We have warned [our British brethren] from time to time of attempts by their legislature to extend an unwarrantable jurisdiction over us."
6. Which of the following does the Declaration use in referring to God? You may have more than one answer. (2 points)
   a. "Supreme Judge of the world"
   b. "Nature's God"
   c. "Father of our Lord Jesus Christ"
   d. "Spirit of Nature"
   e. "Divine Providence"
7. "A right of making laws with penalties of death, and consequently all lesser penalties, for the regulation and preservation of property" is Locke's definition of what? (2 points)

Quiz 2 10 points total

1. Name the term of office for each of the following (1 point each):
   a) Representative

   b) Senator

   c) President

   d) Justice

2. Name one function peculiar to the House of Representatives. (1 point)

3. How many of the State legislatures must ratify an amendment for it to become a part of the Constitution? (1 point)

4. By whom are the following elected/appointed? (1 point each)
   a) members of the House of Representatives

   b) Senators

   c) President

   d) federal Justices

Quiz 3 10 points total

1. Name two of the three provisions in the Constitution regarding slavery. (4 points)

2. Lincoln was "aroused" because the Kansas-Nebraska Act repealed what? (2 points)

3. What did Stephen Douglas proclaim was the principle of the American republic? (2 points)

4. When did Congress first ban slavery in the territories? (2 points)

Section I: Matching (30 points) **Test 1**

On the answer sheet, write the letter of the name or phrase from the second column that best fits with each numbered statement. (3 points each)

1. "zeal for _____ has been found a more certain road to despotism" than "zeal for the firmness and efficiency of government," according to *Federalist 1*.
2. according to Calvin Coolidge, where Thomas Jefferson secured his best ideas.
3. said, "Our constitution... favors the many instead of the few; this is why it is called a democracy."
4. said the Civil War was a test to see whether any nation "dedicated to the proposition that all men are created equal" can long endure.
5. was suspended as part of Coercive Acts of 1774.
6. declared in 1766 its right to make laws for the colonies.
7. made the British Parliament superior to the king.
8. declared in 1774 that the colonies had never ceded their rights to dispose of life, liberty and property without their consent.
9. said that by nature the law is written on the hearts of all men.
10. declared that the people have a right to rebel against tyranny.

A. The British Parliament
B. Abraham Lincoln
C. John Locke
D. Church meetings
E. St. Paul
F. the rights of the people
G. The First Continental Congress
H. Massachusetts' legislature
I. The Glorious Revolution of 1688
J. Pericles, leader of Athens in its glory days

Section II: Memorization (40 points)

Complete the following quotations from the Gettysburg address and the Declaration by filling in on the answer sheet the correct words to fill the blanks. (2 points for each word or phrase)

"Fourscore and seven years ago our fathers brought forth on this continent a new (11) _______________, conceived in (12) _______________ and dedicated to the proposition that (13) _______________."

"... That we here highly resolve that these dead shall not have died in vain—that this nation, (14) _______________ (15) _______________, shall have a new birth of freedom—and that government (16) _______________, (17) _______________, and (18) _______________, shall not perish from the earth."

"We hold these truths to be (19) _______________: That all men are (20) _______________; that they are endowed by their (21) __________ with certain unalienable rights; that among these are (22) __________, (23) __________, and (24) _______________; that, to secure these rights, governments are instituted among men, deriving their (25) __________ powers from the (26) __________ of the governed..."

"WE, THEREFORE, the representatives of the UNITED (27) _______________ OF AMERICA, in General Congress assembled, appealing to the (28) _______________ of the world for the rectitude of our intentions, do, in the name and by the authority of the good (29) _______________ of these colonies solemnly publish and declare, That these United Colonies are, and of right ought to be, FREE AND INDEPENDENT (30) _______________..."

Section III: Choose the best answer and enter it on the answer sheet. (30 points)

31. *Federalist 9* cites ALL of the following as improvements in the science of politics that have made republic government more perfect EXCEPT
    a) the development of direct voting on important issues by the people.
    b) the introduction of legislative checks and balances.
    c) the regular distribution of power into distinct departments.
    d) the representation of the people in the legislature by deputies of their own election.

32. In *Federalist 1*, Publius says, "It has been frequently remarked that it seems to have been reserved to the people of this country, by their conduct and example, to decide the important question, whether societies of men are really capable or not of establishing good government from
   a) accident and force."
   b) zeal for the rights of the people."
   c) reflection and choice."
   d) party opposition."

33. The First Continental Congress claimed that the Americans' rights to life, liberty and property were founded on ALL of the following EXCEPT
   a) the immutable laws of nature.
   b) John Locke's philosophy.
   c) the principles of the English Constitution.
   d) their own colonial charters and compacts.

34. Democratic government in ancient Athens meant
   a) that one faction of the people ruled over another.
   b) that the people ruled through elected representatives.
   c) government of the people, by the people and for the people.
   d) government that outlawed slavery.

35. The principle that taxes cannot be imposed on a nation without representative consent was
   a) invented by John Locke.
   b) the basis of the chief complaint leveled against King George by the Declaration of Independence.
   c) stated in the Bible.
   d) embodied in the relationship between Parliament and the King of Great Britain from the Middle Ages.

36. The Declaration refers to God as
   a) Father.
   b) Divine Providence.
   c) Blind Watchmaker.
   d) Great Spirit.

37. The Declaration charges King George with ALL of the following EXCEPT
   a) refusing to pass laws for the colonies unless they would relinquish their right to representation in the legislature.
   b) making judges dependent on his will alone for the tenure of their offices.
   c) erecting a multitude of new offices to harass the colonists.
   d) establishing the Church of England as the official religion of the colonies.

38. Calvin Coolidge said that the ideals of the Declaration
   a) have their source and roots in religious convictions.
   b) were drawn exclusively from Aristotle, Cicero, and Locke.
   c) were contained in the Magna Carta.
   d) were the same as those of the ancient democracies.

39. According to John Locke, governments are formed by
   a) consent, that is by each man agreeing with other men to join and unite into a community.
   b) the power of punishing unto death.
   c) chance and force.
   d) nature and nature's God.

40. In the Declaration, Congress asserted that separation from Great Britain was a necessity because
   a) all men are created equal.
   b) governments derive their just powers from the consent of the governed.
   c) prudence dictates that governments long established should not be changed for light and transient causes.
   d) the present King of Great Britain is intending to establish an absolute Tyranny over the American States.

Student Answer Sheet for Test 1 **Name** ____________________

Section I	Section II		Section III
1. ______	11. ______	21. ______	31. ______
2. ______	12. ______	22. ______	32. ______
3. ______	13. ______	23. ______	33. ______
4. ______	14. ______	24. ______	34. ______
5. ______	15. ______	25. ______	35. ______
6. ______	16. ______	26. ______	36. ______
7. ______	17. ______	27. ______	37. ______
8. ______	18. ______	28. ______	38. ______
9. ______	19. ______	29. ______	39. ______
10. ______	20. ______	30. ______	40. ______

Section I: Matching (30 points) **Test 2**

On the answer sheet, write the letter of the name or phrase from the second column that best fits with each numbered statement. (3 points each)

1. is what Washington called the greatest interest of every true American.
2. is the source of all laws regarding taxation.
3. were originally elected by state legislatures rather than directly by the people.
4. helps to ensure that no one region or interest can dominate the federal government.
5. was passed by the first Congress to make sure the Bill of Rights would not be taken to imply that the federal government had more powers than specifically given to it.
6. protects the free exercise of religion.
7. protects liberty by sustaining the practical possibility of rebellion against tyranny.
8. has the power to make treaties and appoint judges.
9. demands that search warrants be issued only for probable cause and with details of what exactly is to be done.
10. can only be appointed with the consent of the Senate.

A. The President
B. The First Amendment
C. The Second Amendment
D. The Fourth Amendment
E. The Tenth Amendment
F. Senators
G. The consolidation of the Union
H. Federal Judges
I. The House of Representatives
J. The election of the President by electors from each state rather than by a simple majority of voters

Section II: Memorization (40 points)

Complete the following quotations by filling in on the answer sheet the correct words to fill the blanks. (2 points for each word or phrase)

"The abuse of (11) __________ is a greater danger than the abuse of power." *Federalist 59*

"We, the people of the United States, in order to form a (12) __________, establish (13) __________, insure domestic tranquility, provide for the (14) __________, promote the (15) __________ (16) __________, and secure the blessings of liberty to ourselves and our posterity, do (17) __________ and establish this Constitution for the United States of America." *Constitution*

The Constitution ensures the separation of the powers of government by establishing (18) __________, (19) __________, and (20) __________ branches; these powers reside in the (21) __________, (22) __________, and (23) __________, respectively.

For a bill to become a law, it must first be passed by the (24) __________ and the (25) __________ and then be signed by the (26) __________. But it can become a law even without that signature if it is either not signed for 10 days, or if, having been vetoed by the (27) __________, it is re-passed by both (28) __________ of Congress with a (29) __________ majority in each.

For each state, the number of electors to elect a President is equal to (30) __________.

Section III: Choose the best answer and enter it on the answer sheet. (30 points)

31. The first form of government for the newly independent States was formed by
    a) the Declaration of Independence.
    b) the Constitutional Convention.
    c) the Articles of Confederation.
    d) the Constitution.

32. The Articles of Confederation were established by
   a) the people of the several states
   b) the several State legislatures
   c) the Second Continental Congress
   d) George Washington
33. The Constitution was established by
   a) the people of the several states
   b) the several State legislatures
   c) the Second Continental Congress
   d) James Madison
34. The Articles established how many branches of government?
   a) One
   b) Two
   c) Three
   d) Four
35. Under the Articles of Confederation, who had the power to wage war and enter treaties with foreign nations?
   a) The President
   b) Individual States
   c) The Congress of the United States
   d) Ambassadors
36. Under the Articles, to engage in war or borrow money required the assent of
   a) 7 States.
   b) 9 States.
   c) a majority of the people.
   d) the President.
37. The Constitution places checks on
   a) the legislative power of Congress.
   b) the judicial power of the Federal Courts.
   c) the will of the People.
   d) all of the above.
38. Under the Constitution, Representatives are elected
   a) by the electoral college for a four year term.
   b) by the people of each State for a four year term.
   c) by the State legislatures for a two year term.
   d) by the people of each State for a two year term.
39. Amendments to the Constitution
   a) can be proposed by $2/3$ of both Houses of Congress.
   b) must be ratified by a majority of the States.
   c) must be ratified by $2/3$ of the States.
   d) none of the above.
40. The First Amendment to the Constitution prevents State legislatures from
   a) establishing a religion.
   b) abridging freedom of the press.
   c) restricting the right to keep and bear arms.
   d) none of the above.

Student Answer Sheet for Test 2 **Name** ______________________

Section I **Section II** **Section III**

1. ______	11. ______________	21. ______________	31. ______
2. ______	12. ______________	22. ______________	32. ______
3. ______	13. ______________	23. ______________	33. ______
4. ______	14. ______________	24. ______________	34. ______
5. ______	15. ______________	25. ______________	35. ______
6. ______	16. ______________	26. ______________	36. ______
7. ______	17. ______________	27. ______________	37. ______
8. ______	18. ______________	28. ______________	38. ______
9. ______	19. ______________	29. ______________	39. ______
10. ______	20. ______________	30. ______________	40. ______

Section I: Matching (30 points) **Test 3**

On the answer sheet, write the letter of the name or phrase from the second column that best fits with each numbered statement. (3 points each)

1. held that Popular Sovereignty was the great principle of the American Republic.
2. of 1787 showed the national government had the authority to ban slavery in the territories.
3. "never had a feeling politically that did not spring from the Declaration of Independence."
4. won national sympathy for the plight of blacks by showing the evil of the Jim Crow laws through peaceful protest
5. Ralph Waldo Emerson said of it, "I will not obey it, by God!"
6. outlawed slavery in territories north of 36°30′ N. latitude.
7. denied that Congress had the right to outlaw slavery in the territories.
8. Southern states were forced to accept it as a condition for their readmission to the Union.
9. held that persistent manly agitation was the way to full liberty for blacks.
10. said that the natural condition of the Negro is slavery

A. Alexander Stephens
B. The Fourteenth Amendment
C. Martin Luther King, Jr.
D. Abraham Lincoln
E. The Fugitive Slave Act
F. The Northwest Ordinance
G. The Niagara Movement
H. The Missouri Compromise
I. The *Dred Scott* decision
J. Stephen Douglas

Section II: Short Answer (40 points)

Although you did not memorize any selections from Abraham Lincoln, you should be able to figure out the words or phrases to enter on the answer sheet for each blank. (4 points each)

"All honor to (11) ___________—to the man who, in the concrete pressure of a struggle for national independence by a single people, had the coolness, forecast, and capacity to introduce into a merely revolutionary document, an abstract truth, applicable to all men and all times..." *letter to Henry Pierce and others*

"Let reverence for the (12) ___________ be breathed by every American mother, to the lisping babe, that prattles on her lap...let it become the political religion of the nation..." *Lyceum Speech*

"I was losing interest in politics when the repeal of the (13) ___________ aroused me again. What I have done since then is pretty well known." *letter to Jesse W. Fell*

Douglas tried to avoid national agitation on the slavery question by teaching Americans to say, "I don't (14) ___________," about the existence of slavery in other territories and states.

Legislation passed in 1854 with Douglas's approval overturned bans on slavery in the (15) ___________ and (16) ___________ territories, leading to violent clashes over slavery in one of them.

(17) ___________ laws restricted or denied black participation in Southern public life.

Justice Harlan dissented from Plessy vs. Ferguson decision in favor of state-enforced segregation because he held that the Constitution is (18) ___________.

Today, race is still a factor in (19) ___________ Action laws.

Martin Luther King, Jr.'s, non-violent protest allowed him to educate the American public on Declaration principles, eventually led to the (20) ___________ Act of 1964.

Section III: Choose the best answer and enter it on the answer sheet. (30 points)

21. The Constitution
    a) outlawed the importation of slaves after 1808.
    b) counted slaves as 3/4 persons for taxation and representation.
    c) never used the words slave or slavery.
    d) guaranteed freedom to escaped slaves.

22. How many States allowed slavery at the outbreak of the Revolution?
    a) 4
    b) 7
    c) 9
    d) 13

23. The doctrine of 'Popular Sovereignty'
    a) was established by the Dred Scott decision.
    b) meant that every community has a right to decide whether a thing is right or wrong.
    c) meant that the People should elect its own governors.
    d) was contained in the Missouri Compromise.

24. Abraham Lincoln
    a) rejected all compromise on the issue of slavery.
    b) supported the Kansas–Nebraska Act of 1854.
    c) believed that public opinion and passion prevented the full social and political equality of the white and black races.
    d) urged the federal government to outlaw slavery in the States.

25. The Fifteenth Amendment
    a) guaranteed blacks and other minorities the right to vote.
    b) established governments in the Southern States after the Civil War.
    c) outlawed slavery.
    d) banned the importation of slaves.

26. The decision in *Brown v. Board of Education* (1954)
    a) outlawed racial segregation in schools.
    b) overturned *Plessy v. Ferguson.*
    c) was argued against by the NAACP because it did not treat the Constitution as color-blind.
    d) All of the above

27. Abraham Lincoln held ALL of the following EXCEPT
    a) that slavery is destructive of self-government.
    b) Northerners have a right to defy the fugitive slave law.
    c) the repeal of the Missouri Compromise threatened the Union by re-opening the slave question.
    d) the *Dred Scott* decision had no value as a precedent for other cases regarding slavery in the territories.

28. Which of the following is most likely to have held that the phrase, "all men are created equal," did not include blacks?
    a) Chief Justice Roger Taney
    b) Thomas Jefferson
    c) Abraham Lincoln
    d) Alexander Hamilton

29. According to Alexander Stephens, the immediate cause of the Civil War was
    a) high tariffs on imported goods from Britain.
    b) Congressional restrictions on the slave trade in the District of Columbia.
    c) Abraham Lincoln's insistence on repealing the Fugitive Slave Law.
    d) the South's 'peculiar institution' of African slavery.

30. In Brown vs. Board of Education, the Supreme Court struck down segregation laws because
    a) the Constitution is color-blind.
    b) they caused psychological harm.
    c) they caused economic damage.
    d) they violated the doctrine of Popular Sovereignty.

Student Answer Sheet for Test 3 **Name** ______________________

Section I	Section II	Section III
1. ________	11. ______________________________	21. ________
2. ________	12. ______________________________	22. ________
3. ________	13. ______________________________	23. ________
4. ________	14. ______________________________	24. ________
5. ________	15. ______________________________	25. ________
6. ________	16. ______________________________	26. ________
7. ________	17. ______________________________	27. ________
8. ________	18. ______________________________	28. ________
9. ________	19. ______________________________	29. ________
10. ________	20. ______________________________	30. ________

Teacher's Answer Key for Test 1

Section I	Section II		Section III
1. F	11. nation	21. Creator	31. a
2. D	12. liberty	22. life	32. c
3. J	13. all men are created equal	23. liberty	33. b
4. B	14. under	24. the pursuit of happiness	34. a
5. H	15. God	25. just	35. d
6. A	16. of the people	26. consent	36. b
7. I	17. by the people	27. States	37. d
8. G	18. for the people	28. Supreme Judge	38. a
9. E	19. self-evident	29. People	39. a
10. C	20. created equal	30. States	40. d

Teacher's Answer Key for Test 2

Section I		Section II	Section III
1. G	11. freedom	21. Congress	31. c
2. I	12. more perfect union	22. President	32. b
3. F	13. justice	23. Judiciary	33. a
4. J	14. common defense	24. House	34. a
5. E	15. general	25. Senate	35. c
6. B	16. welfare	26. President	36. b
7. C	17. ordain	27. President	37. d
8. A	18. legislative	28. houses	38. d
9. D	19. executive	29. ⅔	39. a
10. H	20. judicial	30. the number of Representatives plus Senators	40. d

Answers 18, 19, and 20 may be in any order, but then 21, 22, and 23 must correspond (i.e., President with executive).

Answers 24 and 25 may be in either order.

Teacher's Answer Key for Test 3

Section I	Section II	Section III
1. J	11. Jefferson	21. c
2. F	12. laws	22. d
3. D	13. Missouri Compromise	23. b
4. C	14. care	24. c
5. E	15. Kansas	25. a
6. H	16. Nebraska	26. d
7. I	17. Jim Crow	27. b
8. B	18. color-blind	28. a
9. G	19. Affirmative	29. d
10. A	20. Civil Rights	30. b